To Margie
Best Wishes

A BOOMER'S TALE

OR

I AIN'T DEAD YET

Edward J. Piane

A BOOMER'S TALE or I Ain't Dead Yet

Pensiero Press
http://www.PensieroPress.com

Books are available through Pensiero Press at special discounts for bulk purchases for the purpose of sales promotion, seminar attendance, or educational purposes. Special volumes can be created for specific purposes and to organizational specifications. Please contact us for further details.

Cover design by Karen Weidenhoefer
Final production by Gary Rosenberg

Volume 1
10 9 8 7 6 5 4 3 2 1

Contents

To my parents, who greatly influenced my life.
They were my foundation; teaching me integrity, patience,
work ethic, love of God, love of family, and love of country.
They carefully showed us the way to stand on our own feet,
giving us the tools to focus on developing into the citizens,
workers, parents, and friends of whom they could be proud.

Foreword

Timothy Olaska

If this book has a flaw, it is that Eddie is too modest. I've known him since we were aged eight, and he became my hero at 13. He still is my personal hero a half-century later. He does not praise himself, nor does he pull down others to seem better by contrast, as is the current fashion. No, he learned the hard ethics of the streets of Cicero, Illinois and guys like Eddie don't need your praise or admiration. A little understanding would not hurt, however.

This may not be why he wrote this memoir, but it will be your takeaway if you read between some of the lines. You see, Eddie does not see himself as special. And to be honest, his type of guy is not rare. There are uncountable thousands like him, minding their own business, trying to do the best for home and country. Most, like Eddie, have a deep faith, but will not push it on you. No Eddie is not rare, so why read this book?

Because there are so many Eddies out there. They are not asking for sympathy, nor do they seek some other status upgrade. No, understanding and merciful non-judgement will suffice.

My view of this story: Many guys who came back from war left the "service" and set to living their lives in earnest. After seeing so much, they had to come back and deal with much that was mundane, but also forever changed. What changed them was a unique level of stress that only mortal combat can produce. Even those who only saw a little bit of battle have had that stress.

I'm an engineer, not a psychologist. I'm not here to explain, but Eddie is. He will not give you the medical terms, but as you enjoy this book, see the ghosts that haunt all these guys. This is not an explanation, just one life, carefully observed. Take this as raw data, not a theory. I validate much of its contents, having been his life-long friend. I have detected no error in this account.

By the way, it's not all woe. Eddie had lots of fun along the way. He was changed, not broken. He is laugh-out-loud funny at many points. Pay attention to how he says things; he is too modest, as I said, but careful reading by a thoughtful person will yield a great wealth of insight.

How about it? Are you up for a challenge? This book will seem to be a light overview of a life, but with a little pondering and thinking this throughout can gain much understanding. So, please, look into this noble soul and see if you don't understand your own Eddie better.

God bless you, bro!!
—Tim

Foreword

GinaMarie Piane

A funny, candid look at growing up in the 1960s, coming of age in the 1970s, going to war, returning to a changed nation, struggling, and overcoming PTSD, love, loss, growing up and growing old. If you are a human, you will find some part of yourself in this autobiography.

I am the third sister for whom Ed solicited all his friends to pray that I would be a brother. Not sorry! Ed is the oldest and only brother of five kids in a Catholic family. As a big brother, Ed was the type to hold my head under water to see me squirm and scream. He was one part protector, one part tormentor, one part teacher, one part comedian, one part musician, and one part friend. We knew he was paying attention when he was teasing us.

Growing up in the 1960s near Chicago is depicted with wit and charm. Ed introduces the reader to the inside working of the adolescent male mind as he navigates dating and relationship ups and downs. Other Vietnam Era veterans will see themselves in this account and relate to the constant struggle to 'soldier on' when you don't feel like it. This was written at the beginning of what will surely be a creative and productive retirement.

Thanks for the memories.

Love,
Gina

Preface

It was recommended to me, by one of my oldest friends, that I write down some of my life experiences for posterity. I told him, *I ain't dead yet!* (I'm going to try not to swear!) Heck, I haven't even grown up and have no plans to do so in the near future. My friend Tim thinks I'm a funny guy. I have always been able to make him laugh, sometimes spit water out of his mouth if I time it just right. I have been able to make my kids laugh over the years, and now my grandkids (not the teenager of course!) think I'm hilarious. They haven't heard my old stories so it's all new to them.

This is going to be sort of an autobiography. It's not all about me; then again maybe it is, and maybe I'm just making stuff up. You be the judge. And remember, you can't judge what you haven't read. Leave that to our government officials. Oops, did I type that out loud?

Acknowledgments

I would never have gotten this book written without the encouragement, criticism, and enthusiasm I received from my sister Karen. She, being the middle child in our tribe of five, has been both an inspiration as well as a confidant in my head long dive into telling my life story. Karen was the first to proofread my words. If it wasn't for her help with spelling and grammar, no one would be able to read any of this. (Well spell check helped a little.) Karen designed the cover and poured through all the photographs included in this book. Karen also designed all the artwork that has made my current band a minor success in and around Chicago, including our logo and all the fliers I use for advertisement. Karen is so very talented; I just wish we didn't live 2,000 miles away from each other.

I miss her a lot.

Thank you, Karen, so very much for your support, prayers, and love.

Love you,
Ed

Chapter One: The Early Years

I was born in Chicago; well, the hospital was in Chicago. My parents and I lived above a butcher shop, next to a liquor store, and next to a bowling alley in Cicero, Illinois. It must have been a little difficult to get any sleep with my tremendously healthy lungs and a bowling alley with its loudness invading the area. But Mom and Dad were young and in love and they had me. What else would they need? This was 1953. The Korean War was over (they heard I was on the way and all parties started talking peace!) World War II was a bad memory that my father and uncles fought in, but never talked about. People were settling into life, and I was considered a "Baby Boomer." I, of course, had no idea. The only boomer I was slightly aware of came from me, at which time I would again exercise my right to free speech and wake my sleeping parents with my fantastic lung power.

Eleven months to the day after my miraculous entry into the world, my parents brought home another tiny package with another set of healthy lungs. What were they thinking? They had me. It was a lot later in life when I realized that my parents' Catholic upbringing and my father's healthy libido, was the reason it only took 11 months for my first sibling to be born.

Toni and I were almost sort of twins for one month out of the year, December, and at the end of that month, I would regain my status of older brother lording over my younger siblings. Okay, that part was fantasy. I forgot to mention that I am the eldest of five siblings and the only male. I didn't get to lord over anybody. Dad and I could escape by going to a baseball game or the bowling alley. Those were the days when girls were not taken to baseball games with their father and uncles if there was a boy around. That was thankfully me. I got spoiled like I was never spoiled before or since for that matter. My uncles would buy all the goodies (considered junk food today) that I asked for. Even though my father was not the one who purchased any of these wonderful sorts of food items, he sure was in trouble when the next morning I couldn't get out of bed due to a case of the *I ate too much at the ball game.*

He also got in trouble when at the advanced age of around seven-ish I repeated what my dad had called the brown smelly substance left by a neighborhood dog right outside our gate in the alley. My sainted mother did not use such language, at least where any of us could hear. I was lectured by my dad. He explained to me that we never used such language. Then the best part he said, "At least not in front of your mother or the girls." In an instant, I knew the score, and the odds were against us, but Dad had my back.

My sisters, four in all, had many rules growing up ushering them into womanhood. Rules such as: no hitchhiking, no spitting, no swearing, no miniskirts, no smoking etc.; there were a lot of them. The only rule I was given was *Don't hit the girls.* It has served me well over the years and to this day, even at times when I was really tempted, I can honestly say I never hit or abused a girl or woman. Dad taught me well and I'm proud of that. I hope I instilled the same values to my boys, now grown men.

Before our little family moved back to Cicero, we lived on the west side of Chicago at North Avenue and Narragansett. Toni and I had great fun together, playing in the backyard in the sandbox

Dad made. We also walked to a nearby playground. Mom didn't start driving until maybe 1965, but I never paid attention to what date it was in those days. The playground was a wonder for Toni and me in our ignorant youth. Today, Mom would be hauled off by DCFS for child endangerment with wooden swings on iron chains, steel slides that got so hot, you could cook pancakes on them, and monkey bars that were made from painted pipes that reached 18 stories high. I was four years old; they seemed remarkably high to me. And the merry-go-round, pure heaven when the big kids started spinning it at Mach 3.

There were no bumpers made of foam rubber. There were no repurposed shredded tires under these implements of death and dismemberment aimed at small children. We had nice soft dirt and gravel. Skinned knees and torn clothing were just the outcome of another fun day at the park. When we moved to Cicero, we graduated to concrete! The slide was now 18 stories high, and the monkey bars touched the clouds.

At four years old, I could not figure out why Toni would clutch the back of my jacket, or my sleeve when we were outside playing. Yes, we went outside, alone, with Mom inside doing her chores. Toni was badly cross-eyed. Doctors told my folks she would be blind after a while. Mom was not having any of that. She took Toni, with me in tow, to a specialist in downtown Chicago. Remember, Mom didn't drive, so she packed us up and we took busses and EL trains and emerged from the smelly dank underground into the wonders of downtown Chicago. An ophthalmologist named Dr. Cushman gave the family hope. Toni had many operations over the years and never lost hope or her eyesight.

Going downtown on a train was an enormous adventure. We walked by stores with decorated windows, not only at Christmas time, but all the time. If Mom had an extra bit of money, we would get to eat lunch at one of the many cafés in the city in the days before there was a McDonald's on every street. Then we would walk over to St. Peter's Church where Mom would reverently light a candle and pray that the latest treatment would allow Toni's eyes to function properly like the rest of us. I guess they were answered, because Toni would continue to grow and see clearly and develop into one of the smartest, strongest, God-fearing, and loving women I have ever known.

My second sister, Karen, was born in November 1956. Toni and I had a rival for everyone's affection. So, as young children will do, we acted up. We had a parade on the carpet in the living room by which I mean, when Mom was on the phone in the kitchen, we emptied the big can of Jay's potato chips (yes, I said *can* of potato chips, as they came in big metal cans back in the day) on the carpet and marched until the chips stopped making that satisfying crunching sound that Toni so loved. We both climbed into our new little sister's bassinet breaking through it.

We had a big (for a 4-year-old) basement in our building in Chicago. We kids would ride our trikes down there for hours, giving Mom a respite from us and her own *me time* long before the phrase was adopted by today's culture. As a budding mechanic, I learned that machines need oil to make them stop squeaking. I watched Dad use the oil can he kept on his work bench. He learned the merit of putting such items way up high under lock and key so the aforementioned budding mechanic couldn't obtain said oil can.

I commenced oiling our tricycles, liberally soaking the wheels, tires, handlebars, etc., until the oil can was empty and there was an oily autobahn where our small, slick machines traveled. Not possessing the knowledge needed to refill the oil can with fresh oil, I used the only other liquid I knew. I was told never to use the hot water tap to wash my hand in fear I would scald my tiny digits, I deduced that the hot water would not hurt the trikes, or the oil can. For some reason, dad was not amused with us. He cleaned out the oil can and our little racetrack, all the while letting me know that I was never to attempt mechanical repairs until I was older.

He proceeded to show me how to use a hammer and nails on 2x4s that were always readily available in the home of a carpenter such as my dad. More noise, cool. Less cleanup for Dad, again cool. Many, many bruised thumbs, and fingers. I never got the hang of it nor the desire to become a carpenter, like my dad. Turns out Dad didn't want me to have the hard life he himself suffered. Smart guy. I still like big hammers though, nailing, not so much. Now on our monthly trips downtown, Mom had to take Karen, all bundled in blankets (no carriers back in the olden days), carry a diaper bag, one almost blind 3-year-old and me.

I was very curious about, well everything. I asked any question that might pop into my head at whatever time it popped there. "Mommy, why does this train smell like a potty? Why does that lady look like Grandma with brown skin? Will Karen ever be big enough to play with? Why do I have to have sisters and no brothers?" I was a joy to be around.

I can sympathize now, having two sons and many grandchildren.

The questions that come out of their sweet nerve-racking faces. Sheesh! My poor mother. It should come as no shock to anyone that after the first sortie with three of us in tow, Karen and I were carted off to Grandma's house, or Grandma would come stay at our house to supervise our care and safety.

Grandpa never drove a car. He concluded that if he were to drive, he would be required, for safety's sake, not to get behind the wheel of an automobile after consuming his favorite alcoholic beverage. He drank whiskey, wine, (which he made in his basement) and beer. He would never go to work drunk, but came home that way quite often, according to Grandma. So, Dad would either get up super early and pick up Grandma, or get up super early, pack Karen and I into his 1953 Ford. I would stand up in the front seat and Karen would be strapped or duct taped into the damaged bassinet in the back seat.

Seat belts? Ha! We never had them and wouldn't until we were forced to wear them sometime in the '70s. At the rare times Grandpa would ride with us on a trip to Joliet, he would announce just before the car was placed in gear, "Lock-a-da doors, saf-e-ty first." Grandpa and Grandma were from Italy. Grandpa was a plumber toiling many, many years for the railroad.

I remember vividly when I was around three or four years old that I thought it would be interesting to see if I could wash my little cars and trucks. I wasn't tall enough for the sink, so the toilet would do just fine. Of course, I would end up flushing my toys, subsequently clogging up the only toilet in the apartment. Grandpa was summoned. He rode the bus with his tool kit. He came in like a surgeon, no nonsense, serious, and went right to work. He disassembled the toilet to find the offending clog. There were words spoken that would have burned my tiny angelic ears if I had understood any Italian.

I think part of it must have been a curse, because, 60 years later, sweet little Cecilia, age three, flushed a beanie baby and tiny panties. As I disassembled our toilet, saying nasty words in my head, I remembered my own grandpa. I smiled, looked up and said, "Good one Grandpa." My wife thought I had lost it when she came in to check on my progress and saw me smiling and lightly laughing to myself.

My other grandma was from Montreal, Canada. Her first language was French. My grandparents were hard to understand, but they did learn and speak English, and became citizens. Don't get me get started on that subject now.

There were two times in my formative years that I cut myself badly enough to concern my dad when he got home, I was in the care of one or another of my grandmothers. The first incident happened while Mom and Toni were trekking their way to the eye doctor. I insisted that I was skilled enough to make my own peanut butter and jelly sandwich. I had watched Mom. I was 4-and-a-half, besides nobody ever put enough jelly and always too much peanut butter for my discerning palate. I sliced my ring finger and there was blood. I clearly remember the window shaking, baby awakening howl that came out of the kitchen. No, not from me. Grandma was wailing and praying in Italian or Latin and wringing her hands. I was stunned and tried to comfort my grandmother. My cut finger was bandaged, and Grandma took a nap with Karen. I never did get lunch that day. When Mom and Dad got home the ouchy was re-cleaned and re-bandaged. No further doctoring was deemed necessary. I vividly remember starting to weep when Mom removed the bandage to inspect the finger. She told me that if I wanted to grow up and be a doctor, I would have to get used to seeing cut fingers and blood. I remembered staring at my cut finger with all the intensity I could muster. Then said, "Mother dearest, I do not believe I wish to continue my studies to become a doctor. I believe I shall pursue other career options." Okay, maybe not those exact words. (I said I'd be making stuff up.)

The second time for concern was when we lived back in Cicero. My Canadian grandma was living with us, so built in babysitter. I was a street over and was attempting to ride a bicycle that was way too large for me. While navigating the small sidewalk between houses, called a gangway. (I never learned the origin of that term.) I hit the lip of the concrete and plunged into a small basement window, slicing a gash in my left arm on the inside of my wrist. I was worried that I would really catch it for breaking the window if I did not immediately confess. My friend Arnie called his mom who took one look at the carnage, and the blood starting to cover my arm and pants and told me to leave the bicycle and walk right home and have my parents take care of me. "Don't worry about the window," she shouted. (***Translated:*** Please don't sue).

I walked home cradling my arm and catching drops of blood in my baseball cap. When I got home, I called out for my grandma. She came out of her bedroom, again the wails and the wringing of hands and the prayers, this time in French. Then I comforted my grandma, I was getting good at this, walked her back to her bedroom where she lit up a Parliament and drank down a glass of clear liquid that wasn't water. She closed the door behind her. I cleaned my arm, placed three band-aids on it, unrolled a large gauze bandage and retired to the living room to watch TV. When Mom and Dad got home, my arm was unbandaged. Dad grabbed his keys and a towel, and we were hurtling toward the nearest emergency room. I was asked to recount my afternoon adventure, so I did, with all the gory details, well almost all. I left out the part that I was riding someone else's bike that was so big I couldn't reach the ground while on the seat or on the crossbar. Dad was worried about the window.

When we arrived at the hospital, we were greeted by a nun. Yes, we still had nuns in white habits in our local hospital. She had a soothing tone that I did not recognize coming from a nun. My only interaction with Sisters (Shortened to *Strs* in the language of grade schoolers back in the day) was at school. This was different. Okay, I'll trust this *Wife of Christ*, after checking that she didn't have a yardstick.

Dad and I were led into a room with metal tables and the strange smells of the disinfectant used in those days. The doctor came in to examine my now throbbing arm. When he uttered the word *stitches*, I was in a panic. The soothing tones of the sister would not help now. Dad and the evil nun held me down on the table and another nun held my arm for the doctor. I'll never forget the pained look on Dad's face when he looked down into my frightened eyes. It must have been the same look I had on my face when my own son, at three years old, fell down the stairs and required stitches. The major difference was local anesthetic. They didn't use such things on children in 1960; just inserted a knitting needle into a child's, already hurting wound, to sew four gigantic stitches. (We also went to dentists that didn't believe in Novocain, to teach children to brush. All it did was instill a real fear of going to the dentist.) This time the screams and wails came from me. I still had a mighty set of lungs and exercised them to the loudest, lightbulb shattering, paint melting, waking the dead, death metal volume sound ever produced by a sweet little altar boy.

The next day, a Saturday, Dad went over to the next block and helped repair the broken window. Nobody called an attorney, the police nor the media were called. The bicycle manufacturer wasn't hauled into court. The homeowner bought the window glass and my dad installed it. They shook hands and that was that. I was counselled on the merit of not riding bikes that were not mine and too big for me and life went on. I enjoyed a short-lived popularity at school when displaying my black stitches to my awed classmates and I got out of taking a bath for a couple days. Then everything went back to normal; how sad. It wasn't the last emergency room visits for my family. When Mom started driving, she was awarded her own parking spot close to the emergency doors.

For a while there in the mid-1960s, one of us was toted in Mom's station wagon to McNeal Hospital's emergency room. Our pediatricians, two brothers who grew up in Cuba, attended to our various broken limbs, cuts, and contusions. Growing up with grandparents and their accents sure helped us interpret the verbal distinctions of our Doctors Isaac and Alberto Saultiel.

Halloween! My earliest recollection was 2nd or 3rd grade. At Saint Frances of Rome Grade School, it was decreed: "The children can wear costumes to school." That was ok with me. I figured I could trick-or-treat on the way home, drop off my books and start really hitting the neighborhood. Not so fast little Eddie. The next part of the edict was then announced. "All children who come to school in costume, MUST be dressed as either their own patron saint, or an angel." What? No Superman, no tramp, no Casper the Friendly Ghost, no cowboy, not even a ghost? (Well maybe the Holy Ghost.) Okay, Mom found out my patron saint is Edward the Confessor. Patron saint of *difficult marriages*. (I didn't find this out until I did some research for this book, not before my three failed marriages, noooo, I could have prayed: "Yo big Ed, a little help here.") The next part perked me up though. St. Edward was King of England from 1042 until 1066. Dressing up like a king would facilitate my need for free candy on the way home from school.

Toni, on the other hand, had to dress as Saint Anthony, Doctor of the Church, patron saint of lost things. He was a monk. He was dressed in a brown robe with a rope belt. He had a monk's haircut. (Bald on top with a fringe of hair all around his head.) Mom made our costumes, with the help of Grandma. I didn't do too badly; I was a KING. I would parade around in my king attire for at least a week before the big day. Toni on the other hand, was devastated. She had to be a boy saint. She would have preferred an angel or a princess costume. The robe wasn't too bad, but it was the bald wig with the fur glued to the sides, she hated it. She dutifully wore her dreadful costume to school and was praised by the nuns who took her from classroom to classroom showing her off to the other kids, who were giggling behind their hands. I and my king suit, including whatever costume jewelry could be pinned on, and of course my cardboard covered with tinfoil crown, held my head up and sauntered as regally as I could. One nun was starting to chastise me for defying the 'no secular costume' order when I declared "I am Saint Edward the King of England, and I am indeed adhering to the proclamation announced by our esteemed principle." Really, don't all little kids talk that way? I was a saintly king, so I must have talked that way.

Candy was great in those days. They made smaller sized candy to be sure, but not the teeny tiny *fun size* things that are out these days. There was the occasional apple, homemade popcorn balls, and even some fantastic cookies. We never got today's treats. If someone gave us a pencil, or book of stickers, or anything else that was not candy, or something healthy, there would be soaped windows. Okay, that is as bad as we got. No egg throwing for us. (Eggs are food and there were these kids in China that were going hungry.)

I mentioned earlier that our Canadian grandmother came to live with us in the late '50s. Mom needed the help. She was about to give birth again. In those days, it was a crap shoot, but I was rolling the dice for a little brother. I added a special intention to my prayers at night. I also prayed at church and in school. It was a Catholic school, but prayer had not been banned even in public school yet. I talked to my friends about it. "Can you guys put in a good word with Jesus so I can get a brother this time?" No such luck for me. I secretly think Mom wanted another girl so she could save money on clothes. She already had two sets of girl clothes. Hand-me-downs were a way of life back then. I had two older cousins, so, even though I was the only male sibling to date, I got hand-me-downs too.

I wanted a brother!!! We could wrestle and play ball and play war with the other kids in the neighborhood. It didn't dawn on me that even if I were to be blessed with a little brother, it would be many, many years before I could rough house with the brother that I was sure was on his way. My Aunt Yvette was staying with us until Grandma could be moved from her apartment to our house. I was sleeping out on our back porch; Dad was remodeling the guest room for Grandma. Toni and Karen shared a room and Aunt Yvette was in my bed. I was a 6-year-old soon to be seven later in that cold December. I had been praying, so when Mom was carted off, little overnight bag in hand, to the hospital, I was excited. Giddy even. My new brother was on his way.

Early the next morning, Aunt Yvette came onto the porch, sat on the edge of my bed, and proceeded to devastate my little heart. "Another girl??!!!" I wailed and sobbed. How could it be? Did I pray wrong? It wasn't until Dad came home from the hospital later in the day, that I stopped crying. I listened to my dad's wisdom.

"It will be you and me doing things that the girls won't want to do. We can play catch and softball. We can go to games with your boy cousins and uncles. You will be able to play little league." He told me. "You and I can go to the father/son breakfasts at church." Hmmm, that sounded better. I liked all that stuff. When he told me, I would be 12 and almost a teenager when a little brother born now would be six years old, I pondered it and calmed down. My sister Gina was here to stay.

The baseball games mentioned were going to the Chicago White Sox games at old Comiskey Park. I remember root, root rooting for Little Louie Aparicio, (who my grandfather thought was Italian, since he only listened to games on the radio) and Nellie Fox. *Go, Go Sox*! was the battle cry of my youth. That is until I got to high school. Then I discovered the other team in Chicago, on the north side. I discovered Ernie Banks, Don Kessinger, Glen Beckert, Billy Williams, and my favorite player, Ron Santo. I was also a teenager and maybe just a little rebellious. Sorry Dad. My new team was now The Chicago Cubs. I suffered through their losses and there were a lot of them over the years. I suffered when I was informed that the White Sox won it all in 2005. My Cubs finally won it all after 108 years in 2017. *Go Cubs Go!!*

When six years later, Annmarie was born, I was 12 and had my own life and friends and didn't do much more than an eye roll when told of yet another sister. Dad informed me that it was up to me to carry on the family name. I was a naive 12-year-old, who was thinking of becoming a priest. I had no idea how exactly this was to be done. I understood the get married and get babies, had no clue about the mechanics of it. I did know that priests didn't get married and didn't get to have babies. A couple years later, when Toni's friends started coming around and developing into young ladies, I remembered my father's words about the family name. It was an *ah ha* moment for this adolescent, I informed my parents that "I no longer wish to continue my studies to become a priest and shall pursue other career opportunities." See the pattern? The words may not be the same, but it's the way I remember them. Besides, I just could not get the hang of Latin, a prerequisite for a life in the priesthood, thus ending my 2-year stint at Quigley South Preparatory Seminary.

In the summer of 1965, Dad had saved enough money to take the family on our first real vacation. (If you listen really hard, you can hear my sisters rolling their eyes. The story has been told and retold and even turned into a skit we did for our parent's 50th anniversary.)

Dad bought a 1963 Black Mercury Commuter Station Wagon the year before. We had all gone up to Wisconsin for long weekends (fun for us kids, Dad went up to help work on the house of a friend in exchange for us staying the weekend). This was to be a full three-week vacation. We were so excited; we were on our best behavior all spring. The threat of being left behind staying with

Grandma or Aunt Claire was enough incentive for all of us to sit still in Mass, do all our homework, not fight with siblings. My parents wish they could have thought of that ploy years before. Even Santa's naught/nice list only worked a few months out of the year.

New outfits were purchased for all of us. Dad spent hours poring over the AAA maps he sent away for. A small white gas stove was borrowed. The station wagon was packed, and we were heading to California! We followed old Route 66, which none of us kids knew anything about, but Mom and Dad took the same route on their honeymoon back in 1952, so we got to hear all those stories. The 1963 Wagon did not have seats in the *way back* as we called it, and seat belts were not even an option then. Dad being a carpenter, made a backrest for the two siblings whose turn it was to sit back there for their allotted time. (Or when the fighting got bad enough for the wagon to be pulled over, the threats of "We can turn around and go home," then the offending parties were sent to neutral corners and the trip continued.)

The interstate system was not fully complete in those days, so our little family rode on a lot of back roads and through several very small towns. Dad would look for a motel with a pool and we all went swimming before dinner. We all went to bed early, usually right after dinner.

Dad liked getting up before dawn, getting us all packed back into the car, and hitting the trail. He would drive to the next small town after the sun came up and find the local park. We would haul our provisions along with the borrowed cook stove, and pile everything onto a picnic table. We kids would explore the park while Mom made breakfast and Dad read one of the AAA maps that told him how far things were and what our next point of interest might be. Turns out, there were no points of interest any of us kids cared about till the fourth day when we encountered the mountains. This may have been when we all learned that our youngest sibling, to date, was prone to car sickness. Gina was only five at the time, so she can be excused for not remembering much about this epic family vacation. (I think she was just too out of it from the drugs she was given every morning.)

A little perspective. Dad brought $800.00 (mostly in traveler's checks since credit cards were not something Dad used until much later) for a three-week vacation. There were two adults and four children ages 11 down to 5. We drove from Cicero, Illinois to Los Angeles, California and back. We stayed in motels each night. We ate out at least once a day. We went to Disneyland, and several other attractions in Southern California. Dad had the transmission repaired on the way home and a head gasket repaired on the way to California. Dad still had $150.00 left when we got home. There was the time while driving through Ludlow, California that the temperature was hovering between *cook an egg on the pavement* and *the far side of the sun*. Mom was fading. (Mom was also five months pregnant.) I failed to mention earlier that the big black Mercury did not have the air conditioning option. We were all pretty darn hot, sticky, and miserable. We didn't have any juice, or Pepsi in the cooler. There was no water either. Dad had to pay 25 cents for a gallon of water to cool us all off with a drink. Dad told and re-told that story for the next 50 years.

We rolled into Victorville, California; our mighty station wagon was not feeling well. The head gasket on one side of the engine had developed a leak. Dad limped our family transport into a local repair shop to have the necessary repairs facilitated. Aunt Yvette drove out from Long Beach, and drove Mom and us kids, in her air-conditioned car, back to her air-conditioned house. This was heaven. Dad stayed in the desert to wait for the wagon and drove the weary beast into town when it was done. He may have been hot and sweaty, but he had a nice quiet ride. After six days on the road with our noisy brood, this quiet ride must have been his own bliss. He grumbled about spending money on the car, but only a little. We were all together in Aunt Yvette and Uncle Harold's cool house and we were on vacation.

The next few days Aunt Yvette showed us around. She knew all the attractions in and around the greater Los Angeles area. We were taken to Hollywood to see the famous Hollywood sign. We walked down the street with stars on the sidewalk, and the theater where movie stars put their hands and feet in the cement. From there, we were whisked off to see the place where dinosaurs got stuck in the tar and died. Great fun for kids of all ages. The next day we went to see a church made of glass. We had our pictures taken and smiled a lot. Then the beach. Oh yeah, this was totally awesome (if I may borrow a term from today's vocabulary). It was not the actual ocean, but an inlet bay that was calm and had an abundance of sand. The younger girls played in the sand with Mom. Gina was not drugged and played like a regular 5-year-old. Karen would alternate between getting waist deep in the water and playing in the sand. (Karen was-is-and always will be cold, and so was the water.) Aunt Yvette and Cousin Bruce, Dad, Toni, and I splashed and swam in the salty calm water. Aunt Yvette rented us little kayaks. Best day ever, well at least so far. Sunburn! Ouch! We did not have SPF 90 sunscreen in those days. We were all, except for Bruce and Aunt Yvette, scorched. Our delicate Midwest skin was the same hue as a stop sign, and tender enough to keep us in doors the next day.

Now came the day we were all anticipating as if it was Christmas, Halloween, and Easter rolled up in one. Disneyland!!! We fidgeted in our seats. There was no loud talking nor arguing with either cousin or sibling. We oooed and aahed as we approached The Magic Kingdom with Aunt Yvette giving a running narrative all the way there. She knew everything about the place, and her telling us about it made the anticipation almost unbearable. But no one spoke, no one uttered those horrible words of "Are we there yet?" Then we were there. At least we were in the parking lot which was filling up with other families from all over the country and the world. The parking lot was so large, we had to ride a 'tram' to the park entrance. (Tram was a new term for us.)

In those days, there was not an admission fee to get into the park, however, each attraction, ride, and show required a ticket purchased in books. Lettered *A through E*, these books were not cheap. There were lots of A, B, and C tickets, but only a few of the coveted D and E tickets. Aunt Yvette had extras. She had other friends and relations that would visit Southern California and when they left, she collected all the unused tickets for use later. We were all ready to burst with excitement. We entered right next to a garden of flowers in the shape of Mickey Mouse. This was it; we had arrived. There were not as many rides as there are now, but they were all spectacular.

From the *kiddie rides* to the Matterhorn and everything in between, we rode them all. We were astounded by Tomorrowland and all the futuristic things Mr. Disney and his team dreamed up for us. There was a *Video Phone Booth* that enabled a group of visitors to talk with and see another group of visitors at Chicago's Museum of Science and Industry. Magic! How did they accomplish such a feat of futuristic technology? (Here is another generation gap view from the past. All you Millennial/GenXers, and whatever the new term is, GET OFF MY LAWN.)

Our favorite attraction was Pirates of the Caribbean. We got to go on that one twice even though it was an E ticket. We stayed until the very end of the day. There was a fantastic fireworks display, and exhausted, we filtered out of the wonderful magic kingdom, rode the tram back to the car, and the adrenaline charge that fueled us for the day was totally spent. We all had to be awoken and aimed into the house. Pajamas were donned and we mumbled our g'nights. Eyes were closed before heads hit pillows. What a glorious day!

The trip home was not very eventful. The car only broke down two times, and we kids were a tad less angelic. My poor parents. With our vacation in the rear-view mirror, there wasn't anything to threaten us with. Dad drove the northern route home. This meant a seemingly endless tedious highway, across mostly desert in Nevada and Utah. Wyoming and Colorado were a little better with the mountains. Then the flat plains of Nebraska and Iowa. We got a little enthusiastic when we finally crossed the Mississippi into Illinois again. We missed our friends, our dog, and our own beds. We drove out to California as a family in later years. We were older, Dad had help with the driving from Toni, Mom, and me. Our newer station wagon still broke down. We still stayed in motels and ate in little parks in little towns.

Yes, we went back to Disneyland and the beach, but nothing could ever match the first time. That magical wonder of youth was like most things in life, *in the rearview mirror.*

Chapter Two: I'm a Teenager, What Do I Do Now?

I turned 13, three days after Christmas in 1966. Yes, sadly my birthday was right in between Christmas and New Year. I lost out on a lot of presents (I got you this for birthday and Christmas) and parties. On the plus side, I never had to go to school on my birthday, and on the minus side, I never got a party at school or right after school, because we didn't have school that week. No wonder I was such a mixed-up kid.

The 28th of December on the traditional Catholic calendar, was The Feast of the Holy Innocents. This fact was brought up to me by a variety of nuns, yardstick, or ruler at the ready. Except one nun, she who must not be named, carried an architectural ruler. You know the heavy wooden ones with three sides. I blame my arthritic fingers and the fact I can't play the piano on her. Anyway, I was informed about the Holy Innocents, always with that disappointed look and the words, "Why can't you be more innocent like those little boys?" Wait a minute sister. Didn't all those innocent baby boys die a horrible death at the hands of soldiers with big swords? No, thank you. I'll do the best I can with what I have. Let's keep my body intact and all my bodily fluids inside thank you very much.

I was also compared to my sainted sister Toni, who was a straight 'A' student, very studious and modest, organized, and clean, oh and a girl. That's the thing the nuns would never let me or any of the other boys live down. In those days the nuns were the first to discriminate along gender lines. The boys had a strike against them before they even came up to bat. Factor in my perfect sister, and the fact that my mother taught 5th grade at the same school, I could be hit by a pitch and still would not get to 1st base. Hey, that's also the sad story of most of my teenage years with girls too.

I did gain a few points with the nuns when I announced that I was going to be going to Quigley South Preparatory Seminary and would be ordained a priest in the future. Not a lot of points, but a few. My family was very excited to have a priest in the family.

My cousin's wife, Bernadette even went so far as to proclaim that I would be the first American Pope and started calling me Pope Sherman the First. I did a lot of eye-rolling in those days.

Thirteen years old, and in 8th grade! I couldn't wait to get to high school, away from being the teacher's kid and away from being constantly compared to my 'A' student sister. I would be free. I struggled in school. From grade school through high school, I couldn't figure out why I couldn't reach higher than a 'C' average. This always perplexed me. Maybe the nuns were right, and I wasn't gifted with academic prowess. In other words, I was just dumb. At least that is what my ears heard, so I accepted it and sort of gave up. It wasn't until I was a junior in high school (the fact that I made it that far still baffles me) that I figured it out. I couldn't read. Oh, I could read sort of like a 3rd grader, but certainly not at the level I needed to be. This revelation came to me when, for the first time in my life, I got an 'A' in an English class. It was speech class, and there wasn't much reading. I could write a short outline and give a talk and I did great. I was asked by my mother, after receiving my report card, "Why can't you do this well in your other classes?" At which time I (being a teenager) shrugged and muttered, "I dunno," and went out to work on my car or something.

The next semester, I had my epiphany. I picked up, for the first time in my life and not a school assignment, A BOOK. I only remember it was one of a series of books based on the popular TV series *The Man From U.N.C.L.E.* I loved the show, so I picked up the book and started reading. It took me over a month to get all the way through it, (and it was only a small paperback), but I did it. I read my first book. I kept on struggling through a variety of books and finally got the hang of it. The only problem was, I was facing my senior year with a dismal GPA, and I was too embarrassed at the time to ask for help. I got some information by picking up what I could from teachers lecturing in front of the class. I checked out books on LP records (yes, LP records, you young whippersnappers, GET OFF MY LAWN.) from the library to write book reports. I wasn't going to be able to graduate with my class. I was headed to summer school with no guarantee of passing even then. Disheartened with my lack of education, and knowing I wasn't even close to being ready for college, near the end of my senior year, I dropped out and joined The Marine Corps.

I have two friends whom I played with as a child and then we hung around together as teenagers. (Teenagers are way too cool to play!) We still try our best to keep in touch, even when life gets in the way. We are old guys now and Tim is the one who you all must blame for putting a bug in my ear to start writing this stuff down. That was when we recently got together in defiance of the state-mandated quarantine in early 2020. The third member of this exclusive club is Chip. Chip was and is still a free spirit. (Tim is laughing now because we both know Chip was a little nutty.) Chip was a fantastic piano/organ player. When we were still in grade school, Chip would play the organ at church. He was also a whiz at math.

These guys are the brothers I was praying for so hard but ended up with sisters. We had great adventures back then, only a few that involved law enforcement, and a couple that could have ended in hospitals if not the morgue. We were centrally located within walking distance, so we were always at one or the other's homes. We plotted and planned our adventures, though not very well at times.

One day I announced, "Let's ride our bikes out to my aunt's house and camp in her backyard." The guys said "Cool," and the adventures began. My Aunt Molly, my Uncle Joe and two younger cousins lived in Joliet, Illinois. We were in and around Cicero, Illinois. (Tim lived in Oak Park.) Joliet is 40 miles one way. We were 14. Our parents heard this plan concocted by their offspring and said, "Have fun and call when you get there." Not anything like, "Are you three out of your collective minds? That is too dangerous, you'll get murdered, you'll get eaten, or worse, you'll get abducted then eaten." Today's parents would be having us chained to our beds for even thinking of such a dangerous venture. Today's parents would have us all in therapy and drugged for our own good. Not back in 1960 something. So, with our parent's consent, we took off on our trek.

We had three very different bicycles. I had a Sears 26-inch 3-speed that I had saved for all year. Tim had a state-of-the-art, Raleigh 10-speed. Chip had a 1952 Rocket. It was a beast. Balloon tires and a basket in front. It was a girl's bike that his aunt won at a carnival in a time when there were still such things. We rode all day. Thinking we would never make it, we came close to calling it quits. We called each other names that corresponded to various body parts. Most of these exasperated expletives were directed at me, for having come up with this unique undertaking in the first place.

When we finally got to Aunt Molly's, we were exhausted and

starving. Aunt Molly fixed us a feast. She was a fantastic cook, as all Italian women of a certain age are. (Polish wives are fantastic cooks too as can be attested to by my current belt size.) We dutifully called our parents and laid out our sleeping bags under the trees in the backyard. We slept like the dead. In the morning, Aunt Molly made us a huge breakfast and we were on our way again. Even with young fit bodies, we were sore. Peddling was torture, and again with the less than favorable comments aimed at me for the most part. Some were aimed at Chip. He had seen a movie or maybe just the trailer for *Cry of the Banshee* and would at times cry out the title and ad in a maniacal cackle, a falsetto and his own pronunciation (Hear in your head: *Cawieee of Da Banshee.*) We thought it was funny at first and we all laughed. Then it became annoying, then downright irritating. If you have ever been around a 9-year-old who hears a quote from a classmate and continues repeating it until actual child abuse is contemplated, you know what I'm talking about. Ahhhhhh! We made it home without any fatalities. After showering and sleeping for what seemed like a week, we were plotting our next escape.

Later, we planned an ambitious journey that would encompass three states and over a week of peddling. We would bike up to Kenosha, Wisconsin, take a left and head for the mighty Mississippi, crossing the storied river into Minnesota. Take another left and head back through Illinois to home. The trek up to Kenosha was invigorating. We were in our late teens now. I was 17 and Tim and Chip would be turning 17 within the next year. We met up in Kenosha; Tim and another friend Chucky, having left earlier. Chip and I rode up a few days later. The fun commenced. Chip thought he could survive for the 10-day trip with the clothes on his back, an odiferous tarp, and maybe six or seven dollars. He went home with Chucky, and Tim and I set out west. We had provisions, we had money we had saved up for this vacation, and we didn't have the 1952 Rocket girl's bike. I had modified my three speed Sears bike into a racer. New wheels, new brakes, new handlebars, and a direct drive racing sprocket that would not let the rider coast, nor would it enable the rider to gear down for any of the many hills in that part of the county.

Tim had his state-of-the-art Raleigh 10-speed. We slept in ditches on the side of the road. We slept in a barn. We asked permission that time because it was raining, and we got fed breakfast the next morning too. We tried to sleep in a state park somewhere in Minnesota but ended up in our sleeping bags with towels covering our faces trying to keep the bugs from consuming our flesh and carrying us off to their babies. (The mosquitoes in Minnesota are the size of B-52 bombers.) And it was 90 degrees. Best, most miserable night ever. We rode back into Illinois and made it to Rockford and I think it was Tim's state-of-the-art Raleigh that bent an axle. We ended up having to call my father who drove out to rescue us with his trusty station wagon. This was an epic trip that we still talk about today. The details may not be as fresh, but the friendship will last forever. To use a recent ad campaign, *priceless.*

We had other adventures, such as trying to drive to New York over a long weekend and seeing that I was the only one with a license and a car, I had to do all the driving. There was a speeding ticket issued in Ohio. We made it as far as Cleveland. Yes, Cleveland. Not where I would choose to go even for free. Sorry Cleveland, you have a nice city. (I am rolling my eyes, but nobody can see me.)

Then there was the Thanksgiving weekend that we thought it would be fun to try winter camping. We borrowed the faithful station wagon and headed for Minnesota. There was snow. We climbed a bluff overlooking the Mississippi. At least this time we didn't have to worry about the bugs. Possible frostbite, yes; almost getting killed when the car came too close to sliding off a cliff, yes; choking to death from smoke inhalation due to the wet wood we tried keeping lit all night, yes; but no bugs. This was the second best, most miserable night of trying to sleep ever. Oh, and I forgot to mention, I had a nice sleeping bag and a waterproof covering, I also had boots, gloves, and a lot of clothing. Tim had a state-of-the-art down filled sleeping bag rated for absolute zero, a parka, heavy boots, scarves, and other essential gear. Chip had a tarp, cloth work gloves and a hoodie. See, I told you he was tad nutty. Needless to say, we didn't die. The thing about great friends is that even though we lose touch for months or sometimes years, when we do get together, it's like being in a time machine, we are kids again and nobody can ever take that away from us.

I attended my first two years of high school at Quigley, where it was exceedingly difficult hiding my lack of reading skills. I thought at a young age I wanted to be a priest. I didn't know at the time how much a priest had to read, and in Latin too. I could barely read English. Freshman year was a disaster with the constant threat of expulsion, excommunication, and the worst threat of all, repeating freshman year. It wasn't all bad, I learned I was a pretty good athlete. I was small and skinny, but fast. I could swim fast too. I wrestled at the 120lb weight class where I did very well. I ran cross country, swam on the freshman team, and pitched for the freshman baseball team. I didn't do well at basketball. I was a short kid, and never got the hang of not fouling. I also won the intramural billiards' tournament. We were learning geometry and I liked and understood the subject matter. I could visualize angles and shapes, and there was less reading. It helped me be a better pool player.

I also made some new friends. I made some enemies too, mostly because of my friends. (Over 50 years later and I still can't figure that out.) I encountered real live Negros. Don't be offended please. At this time, it wasn't clear what political correctness was. I was taught that Negro was the accepted description of an African American. This was also way before African American was a box to be checked on a job application. I was taught early in life never to use that very offensive word to describe my dark-skinned brothers and sisters. It was during this time, that Negro became Black. Okay, that was easy. I thought Brown would have been a better, more accurate term. Then I thought about being called White; I was a more pinkish beige. There are different shades of brown, so Black would be a lot easier than naming all the assorted hues of brown.

I was raised in Cicero. I only encountered other *races* (Aren't we all one race? The human race? We are just different hues, not different physiologies.) when we trekked downtown or went to the zoo. When Martin Luther King Jr. marched in Cicero, I wanted to go see the march. My father packed up the car and we went to visit our cousins in Joliet. Once there was a realtor who mistakenly showed a Negro couple a house in Cicero. They did not place an offer, they only looked at it and were given a tour of the house. The next day, that house burned to the ground. Sad times back then. That was Cicero, and Berwyn in the '50s and '60s. The '70s were a little better. *All in the Family*, *Sanford and Son*, *The Jeffersons*, and *Good Times* were on TV. We were exposed to the prejudice on both sides of the people of differing hues. We laughed at ourselves while being taught that life wasn't easy for the poor in our cities. The movie *Blazing Saddles* poked fun at all sorts of stereotypical attitudes and bigoted ideas, held by most people back then. I was shocked, when at the end of my two years at Quigley, I came back to Cicero and attended Morton East High School.

The hatred the kids had for all Black people, even though they had never interacted, or ever met any black people was horrifying to me. I traveled 26 miles each way to attend school at Quigley. I encountered hard working people of color on the train and busses I took to and from school. I attended classes, played sports, played music, ate with, and just hung out with a mix of Black, White, Brown, Yellow, and even a few Red. The kids, and some teachers too, were Archie Bunker types for real, and on steroids. I didn't get it and hope I never do. I know only that all people want understanding, not pity, for the past deeds of those who went before us, at least the people I talk with.

The only time I was so very confused was the day Martin Luther King, Jr. was assassinated in Memphis. We were informed while attending class at Quigley. We were dismissed for the rest of the day and sent home. I thought it was out of reverence for the death of a great man, like when we were sent home for three days when President Kennedy was assassinated. I was wrong. My ride home was nothing short of a precursor to my experience in Vietnam. I didn't shoot anybody, so why was I getting such dirty looks from the people on the bus?

When we boarded the train on Western, it was announced that the train would not be stopping until we were past Pulaski. We were also instructed to stay below the windows. I peeked up as we passed the station at Central Park. I was amazed and horrified at what I saw. Buildings were burning, cars were burning. People were breaking windows and looting. When I saw the guns, I hit the floor where I stayed praying for my own safety, all the way home. Trembling as I walked from the bus to the safety of my house, I couldn't wrap my head around the fact that the Black people, justifiably angry over the loss of a great, inspirational leader, would burn their own neighborhood. To this day, no one has successfully been able to explain that to me. I enjoyed having friends that were not from my neighborhood. A couple of these guys were in band with me, and even though I played the bass clarinet, they introduced me to the blues. It was very cool. I loved jamming with the guys. We probably sounded like someone torturing farm animals, but we were having fun. I was ridiculed for my choice of friends, and being short and only 120 lbs., I got picked on and taunted by the kids who thought themselves better than me.

I got in a scuffle or two. Nothing major, until one bully, who shall remain nameless, (we lost touch and he may be a priest) started up with me when I was having a particularly bad day. I tried in vain to diffuse the situation with words. I said "Please kind sir, can't we discuss our differences with conversation and not fisticuffs? One of us may be injured, and if the dean finds out, we could face charges that would restrict our leisure pursuits after classes are dismissed." I'm sure that's how it went. Don't all teenage boys do this first? Yeah, he didn't either. He lunged and, I, being smaller and lighter, (I wish I could describe myself that way today) moved fast, and he missed. Now for the first time in my life, I balled up my fist and let it fly. I had been in *fights* in grade school, but these were mostly shoving and wrestling not actual punching. To his surprise and my horror, I connected. We both started howling in pain. He was on the floor, and I was cradling my hand. I broke his jaw. I also broke my hand; first proximal phalange and the first metacarpal on my right hand. He had to get his jaw wired and subsequently lost some weight. When we healed, we became friends. He was happy with his weight loss, a problem he was battling most of his life, and I was no longer looked at as that skinny, White kid from Cicero. I had earned a small morsel of respect. As they say today, *a win win*.

I had a similar altercation when, in my Junior year, I transferred to my father's alma matter Morton East. At the time I was dressing like Michael Parks who played a motorcycle riding, free spirit in a TV show called *Then Came Bronson*, I just came from a school that required us to wear a tie and jacket to class, and before that we were required to wear cassocks. I loved my freedom of attire. I was also afforded the opportunity to take shop classes. Not much reading, and a lot of hands on. I took welding as soon as I could. Who doesn't like sparks and molten steel? In this class I was not the only new kid. We had a transfer student from somewhere in the south, Tennessee, Kentucky, or Mississippi, I don't recall which, but he had a distinct way of expressing himself. To our Cicero ears, he sounded funny and easy to mock. We were teenagers; it's what we did.

He, of course, took exception to these jibes at his drawl. One day while welding, he accidentally (or not) got a little too close to me with an acetylene torch. I rather loudly called him a non-flattering body part name (see, I told you I was going to try not to swear). The shop teacher came over and asked what was going on. Another student witnessed the conflict and potentially dangerous situation and told the teacher. The offending student with the accent was reprimanded and had to stay after class to review safety practices. He blamed me for this because I spoke up. I was also the shortest kid in the class again.

I was ambushed in the locker room while I was taking off my work shirt. With both hands behind my back tied up in shirtsleeves, I got what is considered cold cocked. He hit me on the side of my head just above my ear. I learned from my previous mistake with fists. I tackled him and this time used my elbow and forearm to bloody his nose and mouth. Two of the guys in the class were football players and picked us both up and separated us before the teacher got there. Someone told him of the fight in the locker room, and he came running. Neither of us were charged with the violent indiscretion because the football players were eyewitnesses and stated that the Southern gentleman fell on one of the benches and I was just trying to help him up. The other kid, not wanting to risk disciplinary action, just nodded. I did too with an angelic smile on my face. Our teacher knew what happened and told me so several years later when we met at the school. I was in uniform this time. When the word got out, I was again no longer picked on in high school. Besides, now I had friends on the football team.

I worked at several jobs during this time; paper route back in grade school; janitor at church on weekends and summer vacation. Then I got a job in the evenings and weekends at a gas station. Yes, a real live, "we pump it for you, change the oil, and check the tires," gas station. I was making $1.75 an hour. I was able to buy my own cool threads. I had to look good for all the girls clamoring to date me. This is where I would use one of those laughing emoji's the kids use on the phone. Even living my whole life surrounded by girls, sisters, and sisters' girlfriends, I had a very hard time talking to girls and had an even harder time asking one to go out on a date with me. I'm told by friends that it was all in my head, and that I did better than most in the girl department.

When I turned 16, a full half year before most of my classmates, and I had a driver's license, I became sort of popular. I could drive a station wagon full of teens to the roller rink. I had a few setbacks, like when a certain cheerleader type coyly asked if she and a friend could get a ride to the roller rink on Friday night. I grinned, "Sure I can drive you; I have the use of a car. I'll pick you up at 7:00 p.m." My naivete came up to bite me, well you know where. After floating around the school for the next three days, I promised my boss at the gas station I would work all day Saturday if he would please let me take this angel to the roller rink Friday night. He, being a man, said, "Sure I'll give you Friday night off, I was young once and I remember wooing girls in high school." (He was from Arkansas, and older so I had to look up what wooing was.) I had my best outfit on. I vaguely remember purple bell bottoms with a yellow double-breasted shirt. (Don't judge my attire.) This was 1970 something, my pants were pressed, I wore a belt, and my underwear didn't show. HEY, YOU KIDS, GET OFF MY LAWN!)

I hardly had any pimples that week. I showed up to pick up my date. Heavy sigh, her friend was her BOYFRIEND. He happened to be grounded from driving due to some infraction of parental edict, probably using too much moose in that perfect hair. Then pouring salt in my wounded ego, they insisted on both sitting in the back seat making yummy sounds back there. When we got to the rink, we parted ways till the end of the night when I was obliged to drive them home, with more yummy sounds in the back seat.

While skating, I encountered a lovely dark-haired beauty. She agreed to skate couples with me and holding hands was wonderful. We exchanged names and where we attended school. Then when the song was over, she didn't let go of my hand. This was nice. We kept on skating in circles and talking about whatever it was that teens talked about back then. She asked how I got here, so I puffed up my chest and proudly announced, "I drove here. I borrowed my dad's car." She was giddy with excitement. It turns out, she was only four months from being able to drive. Her older brother drove her to the rink that night and he and his girlfriend would be happy to dump her off on someone else. Turns out she didn't live far from the cheerleader type.

Things were looking up for this guy. Last skate was called; a couple's skate with the lights down low. Soft slow rock music playing over the sound system. I started showing off my skating skill by skating backwards while still holding hands. On the next straight away, she put her arms around my neck and pulled down and kissed me. Oh wow! Yes, that was my first.

I was a bit flustered to say the least. I fell, she fell on top of me, we slid to a stop. I was mortified and couldn't move or say anything. She said in my ear, "I guess I kiss pretty good, don't ya think?" and then burst out laughing. I was relieved and didn't even flinch when the proprietor yelled at us to get off the floor and leave. Heck, I was amazed we didn't break any teeth or bones and not even my pride was wounded. As we drove toward home, no, I didn't forget the back-seat couple, she snuggled up close to me on that huge front bench seat.

It was then that I learned to drive one handed. The yummy sounds were once again emanating from the back seat. I could feel my face turning red. She seemed not to notice, maybe to make me feel more comfortable. Turning the radio on helped, but not much. Finally, we dropped off the pair from the back seat. They didn't want to get out. They wanted to go for burgers or something. My new sweetheart told them that she had a strict curfew and had to get right home. When we pulled away from the curb, she started laughing hysterically, and said, "I don't have to be home for another hour-and-a-half." I relaxed and we both laughed. We stopped for coffee and talked about nothing for a half an hour. The car was behind the café. We got in and I started the engine. She turned the car off and turned the key to where the radio would play. For the next 55 minutes, there were yummy sounds coming from the front seat.

We dated until I quit school. We would take the EL train into the city, spend the day at the park and walk around the downtown area. We made a lot of yummy sounds all over the place. I got my own car, a 1962 Ford Falcon. It was a real junker, but the guys at the gas station helped me keep it running. (Yes, this is the very same *bucket of bolts* that Tim, Chip and I attempted to drive to New York.) We rode horses in the fall and winter, we rode bicycles in the spring. We did lots of things together. When I met her outside her classroom and informed her of my intention to leave school to join the Marine Corps, she handed me back my class ring, and simply said goodbye. With no explanation, and she didn't want to hear my logic. I was hoping I could have stayed in touch, but no, that didn't happen. Vietnam was still raging, and I told myself it wouldn't be fair to keep her hanging onto someone who might never come home. It may have been that she was just angry with me for leaving school. I guess I'll never know. I was still hurt; that was in March, and I didn't have to leave until September. So, I never went to my own Senior Prom. I guess I didn't do too badly with the girls back then after all. A streak that would not last through my entire life.

The summer before I was due to report for boot camp, I had three jobs. I still had the gas station gig, and I still worked at church though not on a regular basis. I started driving a cab for a suburban company. It was fun and I could make my own hours. So, I was burning the candle at both ends. I didn't have much of a love life, but figured it was just another step heading for the Corps. I was 18 and I was going to be a Marine.

Chapter Three: The Marine Corps Years

I was on the delayed enlistment program, which means that I enlisted in March, but didn't have to report for actual induction and transportation to boot camp until September 4th. So, I earned as much money as I could, but it was never enough. During the few hours that I had in leisure time, I hung around with my buddies and even dated a few times. Mostly, I worried that I may have acted a little rashly in joining up while we were still at war. What was I thinking? I blame it on John Wayne.

I was all gung-ho when I went down to the recruiting office to take the entrance test. Somehow, I passed with a very high score. In those days, when we didn't have photos on our driver's licenses, a recruiter who was short on the number of warm bodies he was to send off to war would sit in the back of a courthouse, and a sympathetic judge would offer a convicted petty criminal the chance to serve his country or go to jail. More times than not, the petty criminal was more than happy to serve his country. These individuals were not the sharpest tacks in their respective boxes. Most couldn't even read as well as I could, not well at all.

So, the same recruiter would pay another recruit, in this case me, to take the enlistment exam for someone else. I was given a license and in hushed tones instructed: "Don't do too good on the test or we will be found out." I was roughly the same size, weight, and eye color as the individual for whom I was taking the test. That is where I thought that things were going a little sideways. My skin tone was not even close to that of the previously mentioned petty criminal. I was then told, "Try to keep your finger over the race part. They don't question what they can't see." I did as I was told and took the test again, missing several questions and this time on purpose. The other guy passed with just a few points above the low mark to pass. I made a few dollars and Uncle Sam got another recruit. I took the test a couple more times, for two more petty criminals. I was then informed that I could extend my leave if I came and worked for the recruiter after boot camp. Calculating the time in boot camp, I figured out that I would graduate boot camp in early December around the 10th. So, wanting to be home for Christmas I said sure, and arrangements were made. Little did I know that I would have to leave home two days after Christmas to report for my new duty station in Millington, Tennessee a day later. Remember the beginning of this chapter? You got it. I spent my 19th birthday in a holding cell, okay it was a receiving barracks, but it seemed like a holding cell in Millington.

If you'd like to know what boot camp was like for me, watch the movie *Full Metal Jacket*. That whole first part set at boot camp was as close as you can get to the real thing. I was always able to do very well in the classroom sessions in boot camp. The instructor read from our handbook or some other manual that was passed out. We then followed along in our own books. Just before we were given a test, the instructor read all the questions and all the answers out loud. This was great. My short-term memory was still pretty good. I aced most all the tests.

The Marine Corps' handbook was the only thing besides the little Bible we were given, that we were allowed to read. I was getting good at reading. I was even drafted into helping teach an individual from rural Georgia to improve his reading skills. I think he had someone take his entrance exam too. He was a very nice guy, but not too bright. I don't remember the name the drill instructors had for him, but you can bet it wasn't flattering. He told me once that this was the first time in his life that he had his own shoes that he didn't have to share with his brother. Now he was in heaven. He had two new pairs of combat boots, gym shoes, dress shoes, and even a pair of shoes to wear in the shower. No, he never said, *Gawaly* or *Shazam*. (You younger readers need to go ask grandma or grandpa what I'm talking about.)

We had our chubby recruits that were restricted in their diet. We had skinny recruits, like me at 130 lbs., who were encouraged to eat what the chubby guys were not allowed to. I was also one of the shortest in my platoon, so I was relegated to the back of the formations. When we ran, I was right there with the rest of the platoon, maybe a little ahead. At the rifle range, I was a particularly good shot. I had never shot a rifle, a pistol or even a BB gun ever in my life. (Never a gun, again refer to *Full Metal Jacket* to find out why.)

My biggest surprise was the day before graduation. We had just gotten through with our final inspection and we were marching across the parade ground. We were told that if we had family attending, we would be able to spend the afternoon with them. The rest of us would be marched back to the barracks to pack up for the trip home by bus. I was flabbergasted to see my very own parents in the bleachers. They were trying to pick me out of the crowd. I informed my drill instructor that my parents were indeed in attendance, so I was allowed to go greet them. We were all dressed the same; green shirts, green trousers, (girls wore pants) black boots, and green covers (never hats). As I climbed the bleachers, I could see both parents looking at the marching platoons. They turned and looked right at me. Then they turned away and pointed to someone that looked like me three months ago. I had grown five inches in height. I now filled out my uniform in the chest area and gained 37 lbs. of mostly muscle. When I got right up to them, I had to call their names to try to get their attention. Since there were a lot of calls of "Hey Mom and Dad," my calls were ignored until they were close enough to touch. Dad did a classic double take and grabbed Mom's arm. I towered over both. Mom cried and hugged me. Dad didn't learn to hug for several more years. In the *Greatest Generation*, men did not hug one another, unless drunk, or as the term back then was *light in the loafers*, or *a confirmed bachelor.* Men shook hands. So, we shared a hearty handshake. I was no longer a little boy. I was a man. I was a Marine.

At home on leave, I was a star in the neighborhood. I walked over to Mom's classroom and impressed her 5th graders. I refrained from sneering at the nuns I used to know and fear. I was polite and realized they couldn't smack me with their rulers anymore. I walked down to my old high school. Morton College was ensconced in the top floors of the Morton East High School campus until the new building was constructed a few miles away. There were some familiar faces from the class I should have graduated with. I was pawed by a few young ladies and given a wide berth by a few of the guys I used to know. It was all over their collective faces. Where is that skinny kid with the stocking cap forever perched on his head? All in all, I was a star. I was not yet 19, but when I tentatively entered one of the many local taverns in town, I couldn't buy a beer. I had several bought for me and the bartender was told, "If dis guy can put on dat uniform and fight dat war wit da commies, he can darn well drink a beer in here." I was a star.

I attended Aircraft Maintenance School down in Tennessee, most of which was a hands-on classroom/shop class. I did well and enjoyed it. The classroom portion was also easier than any book learnin' (I'm in the south now) class I ever attended except for boot camp. One thing that was drummed into us was that if we failed this school, "There is a rifle waiting for you, and a whole lot of gooks out there who will be shooting at you." In other words, if we failed, we would be transferred to the infantry and shipped off to Vietnam where the local population would be doing their best to end our existence by shooting at us. Talk about motivation. Another way of being shipped out to a grunt unit was to go to sickbay and complain about a non-existent malady, one most likely caused by the consumption of alcohol, which could have the same effect as failing. That individual in question would more than likely be ordered to start the school cycle over. We were effectively motivated to study hard and pay attention in class and deterred from going to sickbay.

Towards the end of school, with only two weeks left, I became ill. It was not an alcohol induced illness. I was sick but determined to finish with my class. I slept as much as I could. I tried to eat, but had no appetite, I had a wicked sore throat, and I was tired all the time. I was pale and frankly didn't look too good.

On the Thursday of this same week, I was in the classroom listening to a lecture. (The rest of this was transmitted to me by a couple of my classmates after the fact.) I nodded off at my desk. After several attempts to awaken me by yelling expletives very loudly and even tossing an eraser my way, the instructor came over and less than gently nudged my chair. I proceeded to fall out of said chair and lay on the floor. The instructor, a seasoned Marine, had all the color drained from his face and his eyes looked as though they would pop out. I passed out cold. An ambulance was summoned, I was loaded off to the base hospital. The instructor was offered oxygen. I awoke three days later, on Sunday afternoon. My own snoring brought me around. The first thing I heard was coming from the next bed. "Thank God he's awake. Any more of that snoring and I would have smothered him." I was so hungry, but remarkably refreshed. I was told I had Strep throat that had developed into Mononucleosis. Because I didn't want to have to start the school cycle over, I ended up in the hospital. I only missed one day of class and, because I did well in class and shop, and I obviously was not faking it, I was allowed to finish with my class.

During my stint at school, we could enjoy the enlisted club on base. We could listen to music and consume alcohol. There were women there too. This was a Navy base, so the enlisted club was filled with Sailors and Marines, some of whom were female. These were not the cheerleader types nor were they the cute little girls we were used to dating back home. There were Waves and WMs: Women Navy personnel and Women Marines. The latter was commonly known by a certain body part that was sung about by the rock group Queen. We referred to these WMs with the acronym BAMS or big ankled Marines. (Substitute ankle with a less flattering body part a little north of the ankle. Sung about by Queen in their song *Fat Bottomed Girls*.) After a few alcoholic beverages, the two genders would mingle. More drinks were consumed. Pretty soon couples would filter outside to dark secluded places on base and make some yummy sounds. This may have been where I contracted my Strep throat, or maybe my Mono. Anyway, it was fun and didn't lead to much more than light touching of female body parts normally relegated to feeding babies and of course the yummy sounds. Life was good in the Corps so far, and I was only 19.

After school, I was sent to New River, North Carolina to report to a real squadron. I knew New River was a helicopter base, but I didn't know to which squadron I would be reporting. When I was sent to HMA 269, I was elated. This was an AH1J Cobra squadron. The coolest, baddest attack helicopter in the U.S. arsenal. This was 1973 and the Apache had not been put in operation yet. However, I was not the star I was back home. I was the new guy. I got all the less desirable jobs and was hazed like new guys all over the world were and still are hazed. I was sent to other shops to borrow an extension cord for a drill when we only used air drills. Sent to another shop to ask for 50′ of flight line. And the classic sky hook.

Another haze was called the hammer qualification where a new guy would sit cross legged on a concrete floor. A small circle was chalked right in front of him. He was given a ball peen hammer and told he was to hit the circle as many times as he could in a specified time. "Sounds easy, right?" He nods. Then he's told he must be blindfolded. A little less easy, but he couldn't refuse. After all, he was a Marine, and always up for a challenge. Bets were made, taunts were issued from the more seasoned in the room. Stifled giggles emanated from behind hands. A blindfold was placed on the new guy's head after first surrendering his cover to one of his shop mates. A stopwatch was produced, the senior Sargent in the room yelled go, and new guy started hammering as fast as he could. At this point the new guy's cover, (hat for those of you that weren't paying attention earlier) was placed either in the small circle or wherever the hammer blows were most concentrated, thus causing the aforementioned new guy to totally obliterate his own cover. When the blindfold came off, the circle of men spread out quickly. (New guy had a hammer in his hand.) Much laughter ensued and some rather impolite curses and name calling exploded from new guy's throat. (Name calling and cursing often referred to body parts, what unnatural acts no one could possibly perform on oneself, and often referred to the sexual preferences of everyone's parentage.) When new guy calmed down and was relieved of the hammer, he was patted on the back, his hand was shaken, and he was proclaimed as "One of us now" and handed the bet money collected to buy a new cover and have a couple beers on the shop. Now new guy couldn't wait for the next new guy to arrive.

The pilots of these attack helicopters were all officers and were supposed to be gentlemen. Most were fine Marines that were enthusiastic pilots, and they did their jobs well. These officers also knew the value of their enlisted men that kept their birds flying. A few needed a little more education in *How to treat the guys who kept your bird from falling from the sky*. You would think there would be a mandatory class at flight school covering this. Maybe these few officers were out sick the day it was covered. No matter the reason, these guys were real hard cases. So, we in the shops devised a few training lessons that were not harmful to the pilot but got our point across. The one that was very effective involved the pilot relief tube. As the name indicates this was a device that allowed a pilot who was confined in a cockpit for long hours to empty his bladder without having to land his Cobra. Larger helicopters had a small head for the same purpose. If a particularly unpleasant pilot was deemed to require an attitude adjustment, a small rivet or screw was placed part way down the relief tube. The adjustee, after attempting to empty his bladder, would have a warm feeling inside his flight suit. I'm sure there were words spoken unbecoming of an officer and gentleman in said cockpit.

On landing the soggy officer would be taken aside by a senior officer and informed that he had been given a warning. The chastened and now re-educated pilot had a higher respect for the men keeping him from falling to earth surrounded by flaming wreckage. Helicopters do not have ejection seats and they don't glide at all. When an engine stops working, they tend to drop with the same aerodynamics as a truck falling from a great height. We in the shops often received an apology from the kinder and gentler pilot, and a stern dressing down (mostly tongue in cheek) by one of our senior NCOs with a "Let's not have this happen again." It didn't happen again (. . . until we got a new batch of pilots.)

Jacksonville, North Carolina was an awakening for me. I learned new things and met new people. I learned a new language; the words were fairly close to the mid-west English that I was taught as a child. I learned that the term *y'all* directly translated to *yous guys*. Then there are several conjugations concerning *Yonder*, this is used instead for *over by der*. Food was interestingly different too. Grits were served at breakfast unless specifically requested to be held or substituted for *taters*. Pork chops were on the breakfast menu in most of the local eateries. Also, ham was on breakfast menus. You either ordered *Country ham*, or in some places you could get *City ham* which was not very salty and could reasonably be eaten without the eater's blood pressure skyrocketing to the *off the chart, call the cardiac unit* end of the spectrum. Then there were greens, collard, turnip, and mustard. I sampled all of these and was not repulsed, most of these were after all simmered with bacon.

I learned the art of peeling freshly boiled and cooled shrimp when I was invited to dinner one night at the home of a nice older couple. They had a son and daughter, both teenagers, and we sat down to eat. There were greens and boiled taters, and an empty bowl at each place setting. Grace was offered by the dad, and a huge bowl of pink crustaceans was placed in the center of the table. There was a frenzy of activity, and little pink shells were filling the empty bowls all around the table. Except mine. I was mesmerized at what was happening in front of me. My mother would have passed out with the sight of the peeling and consumption of food without the aid of utensils, just fingers. When it was observed by the lady of the house that I was not indulging, she told everyone to stop. They stopped after her tone and volume were tested for a third time. I was now instructed in the fine art of peel and eat shrimp. I wasn't too fast at first, but I got the hang of it quickly and this was a feast.

Dessert was another southern delicacy that I had never tasted before. Fresh Pecan Pie. Be still my heart. With just a single scoop of hand churned ice cream on top it was an explosion of wonderfulness in my mouth. Belly full, my taste buds doing a happy dance in my mouth, I thanked my hosts silently praying I would be asked to return. I was and the next time I was a little faster. I was also treated to a new dessert that was every bit as spectacular as the first: Banana Pudding (pronounced *puddin'*). It's a real good thing I left the East Coast when I did, or I could have developed a rather sizable mid-section. (It took a long time to develop the larger waist size I now possess, and I earned it.)

I would try to find cheap airfare from North Carolina to Chicago in the days when military personnel could fly stand by and be placed ahead of any others who wish to wait around to see if there would be a seat available to their preferred destination. I did so as often as my paycheck would allow me. I would leave the base as soon as possible on a Friday and take the last red eye back on Sunday night, or in the case of a holiday, Monday night.

The logistical problem came up when I realized that the only Airport in the entire area, maybe even the state, flew out of Raleigh/Durham which was 135 miles away. So, I would pack as much stuff as I could on my 1972 Honda 450cc motorcycle and get to the airport 15 to 20 minutes before the plane was due to hurtle skyward. Thank God this was way before the recent restrictions on air travel were put in place. I would have never had a chance to go home for long weekends.

On one of these occasions, my sister Karen introduced me to a young lady in her social circle. We got along very well and became a couple in no time. Now I was even more motivated to take that silver bird home. I know what you are thinking and yes, there were plenty of yummy sounds.

She was a senior in high school and thought it was just the greatest thing to have a real live Marine as her boyfriend. We even attended her Senior Prom. I was resplendent in full Dress Blues. I was a star again. I was introduced to all her girlfriends who just seemed to melt and turn green in front of our eyes. The boys gave us a wide berth and glared at me. These were probably the same long-haired hippy types that spat and called names in airports in later times. I didn't care, I glared right back. There were no confrontations, and we had a great time.

As our love blossomed, I bought a ring and proposed. This was after she graduated of course. When I was home, we spent long hours talking and making plans like all young couples did and, I assume, still do. We didn't talk on the phone very much because it was quite expensive. This was way before the advent of unlimited talk and text on cell phones. Those terms were not even an idea on anyone's radar, well maybe Gene Roddenberry. We wrote actual letters on real paper, placed them in an envelope, and entrusted them to the U.S. mail. Life was good.

There were a few instances when returning to the *Tar Heel State,* the roads were almost impossible to navigate due to a dense layer of fog that made the roads (no highway, or expressway yet) disappear. At these times I would find a safe place to pull over and take a nap while perched on top of my bike. I would drape a blanket over myself and retain as much of the engine heat as I could. I would awaken in the wee hours as dawn made the roads visible again and get back to base as fast as my little two-wheeler could propel me. Thankfully, I never got stopped by the state or any of the local police as I streaked along. I was never late for muster either. There were a few sleepy days when I would find a nice quiet place in a hanger or in a helicopter and stole a little nap, but not too often.

Then the orders came. My orders came. I was being shipped to the other side of the world. I was being transferred from HMA 369, to HMA 269. Japan? Oh, why me? I had a fiancé at home. Well, when the Marine Corps says jump, all you can do is say, "Aye, aye sir. How high sir?" And follow orders. She was sad of course, and as I spent my final days at home making the most of this precious time. We both promised to be faithful. We promised to write every day. We would be together again in no time. We said our farewells and that was that.

Chapter Four: Dear Ed...

I was whisked across the globe to Marine Corps Air Base Futema, Okinawa. Now this was what they called culture shock, not to mention the worst jet lag I have ever experienced. By now it was 1974 and Vietnam was winding down; at least that is what the scuttlebutt said. (Scuttlebutt was the word used in the ranks, to refer to *mostly* rumors). I learned to eat with chopsticks. I had to if I didn't want to carry around my own fork or go hungry anytime

I left the base. Fried rice and Yakisoba were usually the cheapest things on the menu at any local café. Not the easiest things to eat with chopsticks, even for the more seasoned Americans in the Far East. Eventually hunger overcame lack of skill, and I began shoveling exotic Asian delicacies into my watering mouth.

Okinawa was hot and humid; hotter and more humid than I had ever experienced in a Cicero summer or even in my time in North Carolina. Clothes never seemed quite dry. Sheets never seemed quite dry. Our use of deodorant doubled and, in some cases, tripled. Then as soon as we got used to the weather on Okinawa, my squadron was sent to the Philippines. This was February and Okinawa was getting bearable. It was 110 degrees when we landed at Cubi Point Air Base, Philippines. The humidity was also hovering around 110%. We got off the plane and we were wearing serge green utility uniforms and field jackets. It rained the first time we were able to leave the base and venture out to explore the local village, just a stone's toss from the main gate. The rain was hot, but the most interesting thing was the fact that we were getting wetter from the steam rising from the pavement than from the light rain falling on us.

This was a time of Marshall Law in all the Philippines. Ferdinand Marcos was President, and his wife Imelda was buying out shoe stores all over the world. Everyone, military and civilian, had to be off the street by midnight. ***Note:*** this is where we get the term in military circles of *Cinderella Liberty*. Instead of turning into a pumpkin, you could get yourself tossed into the brig. Or in the case of the Philippines, tossed into the local jail. Thankfully, I never saw the inside of one of these local establishments. Except for the week, I was assigned to the MPs (military police) accompanying these MPs and SPs (shore patrol) to retrieve whichever of our fellow Americans failed to make it back to base before midnight. The more grievous offenders of the local law needed more time to reflect on their conduct. Most of this latter group would also need a good lawyer or at least a lot of bribe money. Nobody cared whether you went back to base or found refuge in town, as long as you made it back to base by morning muster.

There were a multitude of young ladies (most ladies of a certain old profession) that were happy to have an equally young Marine or Sailor take refuge in their very humble abode to save them from being detained by the local Gendarme. Yummy sounds could be heard throughout the city. These soiled doves did ask for help to supplement their meager income earned by waiting tables, or serving drinks, or dancing at the local watering holes. They were now girlfriends that took care of the young Marines and Sailors hoping for the chance to be sent for when the young men returned to *the states*. Some did in fact make it to the states and some are still married to the no longer young Marines and former Sailors. The currency at that time was about eight to 10 Pesos to one American green back. So, our money went a long way and we lived like kings.

I was engaged; so, I was back on base before midnight at least until I received THE LETTER. I must first point out that I left the states in August of 1974. This was March of 1975. I was informed that my fiancé was with child. I was further informed that she was a little over five months into her confinement. (Check the Bible for that reference.) I counted the months on my fingers. I've never been what would be referred to as a math whiz, but I concluded that someone had been making yummy sounds back home and it wasn't me.

Yes, I was very hurt. I was confused, what do I do now? I waffled back and forth. Do I forgive and raise a child that wasn't mine? Do I end the relationship? I went to the chaplain. Father Brian was a Catholic priest stationed at Subic Bay Naval Base. The Marine Corps doesn't have its own chaplain, so we enlist the services of Navy chaplains. Fr. Brian gave me the standard "to err is human, to forgive is divine" statement. Then he said, "Ed, my son, let that trollop go, if she can't wait for a man for a year, she's no good for you." You must understand, I encountered Fr. Brian in Boot Camp. He was an Irishman and had a pronounced brogue. It seems he was sent by God and, the Marine Corps, to follow me to several duty stations. I took his advice.

When I got the letter, from the trollop's stepsister, I knew I had made the right decision. This latter letter outlined the specifics of when one of my supposed friends started coming around to look in on said trollop. Saying his visits were sanctioned by me, the parents didn't think anything of it and considered it a nice gesture. When they were informed of the confinement of their daughter, they too did the math. This is where they encouraged the sister to write to me. In the next post, I received my ring back which I sold in town to a pawn shop. Now I had no restrictions that kept me sequestered on base when the midnight hour came around.

Not going into detail, but there was alcohol involved. Maybe an entanglement with a young lady who, not being a great English speaker, was a very good listener (not that she understood my words, but she did get the meaning, at least she nodded and smiled.) As long as I was buying the drinks, all was right with the world. Okay, maybe there were some of those fabled yummy sounds too.

After several exhausting weeks on shore, (exhausting due to the Cinderella Liberty mentioned earlier) we were herded aboard our respective ships and went to sea. We were heading for Vietnam. Hey now, we were told that the war was over, what gives? Turns out the war wasn't really over yet, and we were heading to the Gulf of Siam near that particular Southeast Asian country. I am not going to go into detail about the war right now. Maybe later in the book. I'll just say I participated in **Operation Eagle Pull** (the evacuation of our personnel in Phnom Penh in Cambodia) and **Operation Frequent Winds** (the evacuation of the U.S embassy in Saigon, Vietnam currently known as Ho Chi Minh City). I was involved in several sorties in a country where we retrieved remains of fellow service men. And later the retaking of the U.S. ship Mayaguez, after it was taken by Cambodian pirates.

When I made it back to Okinawa, I was introduced to Chrysler Military sales. Wow! I was going to buy a new car. I knew Dodge was part of Chrysler and ever since the Charger came out, I wanted one. The problem that shattered my dream of owning a brand new Dodge Charger with all the options I could imagine, came when I entered the sales office and discovered to my horror that some pencil pushing idiot decided to change my beloved Charger to something that looked more like a *family, go-to-church car.*

I was not amused. I couldn't buy that car. It wasn't sexy. It wasn't stylish. It was something my grandfather (if he were to drive) would have been happy owning. I decided if I couldn't have an expensive cool car, I would buy a much less expensive practical car. So, I bought a brand new 1975 Dodge Dart Swinger. I ordered none of the fancy options I would have gladly paid for in a new Charger. I ordered the basic car. Maroon in color with a 3-speed manual transmission with a column shift, bench seats, and an AM radio. I did have Ziebart undercoating applied, but nothing else.

I picked up my new car when I returned to Cicero and drove it back to North Carolina. The car was possessed by demons. Maybe just a magnetic field that attracted trouble. Okay maybe I had some fault in the matter. I did rear-end another car that was driven by a local official's daughter who also happened to be the reigning Miss Onslow County.

As a single Marine, I was always on the prowl for a nice young lady for companionship. You know, like going to the soda shop or Bingo night, or maybe a church social. Ha Ha Ha. This was 1975 and 1976, not 1956 or *The Gomer Pile Show.*

The biggest problem was the fact that when a daughter was pretty and possessed a good figure, this daughter's father would ship her out-of-state for school. Frustrating for a young Marine searching for love. The second biggest problem was the fact that there were the other 50,000 marines also stationed around Jacksonville and the young civilian males who have been court in' the young ladies in the community since they were in grade school. So, most of my leisure time was spent fishing, or riding motorcycles, or hanging around (In those days we hung around, we would never *hang out* like they do today.) with other young single Marines talking about girls we knew back home or overseas and remembering the yummy sounds. Mmmmm.

I had my radio (a CB radio; it was 1975 after all) and everybody had or wanted a CB radio. My radio was stolen out of my car three different times. One time I was on leave and my car was sitting in front of my parents' house, still in Cicero. I couldn't begin to remember my call numbers, but my handle was *Fast Eddie*. Everybody had a handle, the cornier the better. There was the *Pink Panther*, a grizzled retired Marine and his wife, *Pink Petticoat, Carolina Blue* and her husband, *Carolina Bull Dog. Jack-O-Diamonds, Gumball, and T-Bone* were some of the single guys. (This was way before I drove a truck and had the CB in my face all the time.) These were a group of local civilians and retired military who were very friendly to us young Marines. We were invited to picnics, parties, or just out for a drive in the country in *convoy* fashion, all the while talking on the radio, cracking jokes, and pointing out landmarks and other points of interest in and around Jacksonville. We would then have dinner either at a local greasy spoon or the home of one of the married couples. These were the best because of the fantastic desserts that were always homemade and always served in large portions.

After my 1st enlistment was over, I re-upped. I was now a Sergeant E5, and my next duty station was to be in California. This was cool with me because I had connections in California. My sister Toni was newly married and lived in Whittier with her husband Dale. I had my Aunt Yvette and Uncle Harold who lived in Long Beach with my cousin Bruce.

After driving it to California, I lent my car to a good friend who I was sharing an apartment with. I was heading for a 2-week cruise aboard the USS Tarawa for additional training, and I let my friend drive my car from the base in Orange County to our apartment in Long Beach. As he was pulling into our complex's parking lot, he managed to get into an accident smashing the right side. I was not a happy camper when I returned after the cruise expecting to find my friend waiting WITH MY CAR, so we could drive back to Long Beach. No friend, no car. Suspicion started clouding my mind. My fears were realized when I inquired of an acquaintance of both of us, the whereabouts of my friend and my car. He said, "Oh didn't you know? He was in an accident and wrecked someone's car." That someone was me, and the car in question was mine. I did not ask about my friend's health. I did ask about his whereabouts. I was informed that he caught a ride with someone else and was probably at home. I had to call my sister to drive me home where I found my roommate in an advanced state of intoxication cowering in our apartment. The apologies and pleading started. He was so pathetic I couldn't help but to burst out laughing and join him in furthering his inebriated state. We are still friends. I did make him pay my deductible and we can still laugh about the incident today. I will have to ride down and visit him soon.

Chapter Five: I'm Going to Be a Daddy

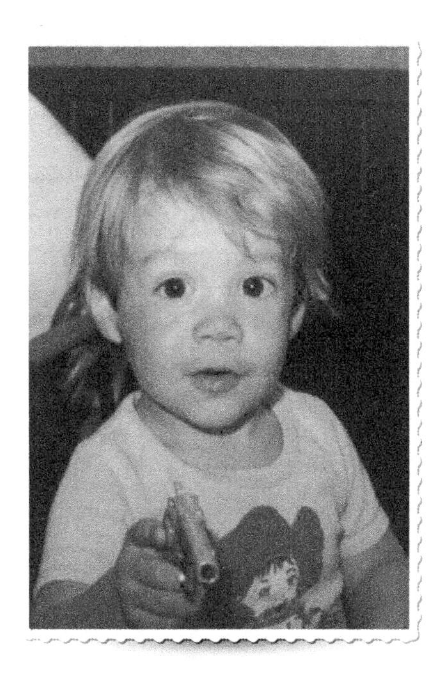

Life was good. I hung around with kids from Cal State Long Beach where Toni was still enrolled. I met a lot of good friends that I am still in contact with today. I met my first wife at a Newman Club meeting/church service. After a yearlong engagement, we married, and a year later my first son Gabriel was on his way. Then things went sideways, when she was pregnant with Gabe. (We didn't know the gender yet; it was 40 years ago, the stone age.)

I was informed by my Marine Corps that I would be once again deployed back to the Far East and back to Okinawa for 13 months. I wasn't happy, but she was outraged. She demanded I plead with my commanding officer to let me stay home with her. She was having a baby! Couldn't the Marine Corps make an exception for her? The Marine Corps is a lot of things, but compassion for a spouse is not in the handbook. The saying goes, "If the Marine Corps wanted you to have a wife, they would have issued you one." I shudder at the type of wife the Marine Corps would issue. The only concession made was a 1-month delay so that I could be with her when my baby was born. That was great!

It just so happened that my parents came out from Illinois and were visiting Toni who had given birth to my first niece Kristen five months earlier. My grandmother (Dad's mom) was also with them for the visit. I had taken a week's leave knowing that the blessed event was near at hand. I didn't know how soon it would be so I had our station wagon (I bought the well-established Piane family conveyance) in pieces in our driveway when at 6:00 p.m. who should come waddling out on the back porch but my very pregnant wife announcing that, "I think I'm in labor." Oh great, my other car was a tiny Triumph Spitfire that would have taken a small crane to get her out of, that's if I could have shoehorned her into the tiny roller skate of a car in the first place. I feverishly worked on the trusty station wagon. And in record time, I had it together.

It was now around 9:30 p.m. at night (21:30 if we realize I'm still in the Marine Corps at this point) and off we drove to the Orange County hospital. We were way too far away from the nearest military hospital in Long Beach. When we got there and we had her all signed in, I phoned my sister's number and announced to the family that the birth was upon us. At this point it came to me that I had not consumed any sustenance since breakfast. I must have informed my sister of that because when they arrived, I was given two ham sandwiches and a Coke made by my mother. (The sandwiches, not the Coke.) How did they taste, you ask? I don't know, I think I swallowed them whole. One catastrophe averted.

I then went to my wife's room and sat with her, and sat with her, and sat with her some more. Where was our little bundle of tax deduction? Was this supposed to take this long? I asked the next person in a white coat that I saw, and was informed, "Sometimes it takes a while dear." I had been up since 5:00 a.m. (05:00) and I was working on a car all day. I didn't want to hear that it would take a while. Sometime around 4:30 a.m. a different nurse came in and looked at her chart and examined the relevant area of my wife's anatomy. When the nurse stood up, she looked at the chart again and had a grim look on her face. I saw the look, but my wife did not, thank God. I followed her out into the hall, where I found her on the phone asking someone to send up a pediatric surgeon. (Not sure if that's the right term for the guy who does Cesarians, but that's the way I hear it in my head 41 years later.)

Now I was starting to get a little freaky. What was happening? Of course, no one could or would tell me anything until the doctor arrived from somewhere in the bowels of the hospital. When he did arrive, I nearly tackled him, but he brushed past me to check the chart and examine *down there*. When he came up for air, we were informed that the baby was in distress, and they were going to have to perform an emergency C-section. Okay, we knew that such a possibility could arise. We were prepared. I was going to be there. I was rushed out to be scrubbed, I was given a gown, booties, and a hat. I was given a mask and was told where to meet the doctor. The doctor took one look at my disheveled, and sleep deprived self and stated, "I haven't lost a father to date and you sir are not going to pass out in my operating room." I protested, but not too long, (just enough to keep up my macho image, in my own mind). I removed the paper garments and joined my family chatting in the waiting room.

A lot of bloodshot eyes (mine being the worst) stared at the clock. Toni and I were just walking past the receiving window, when she asked how I would know when the baby arrived. I was just then looking at a tiny bloody naked baby boy and I turned to Toni and said, "There he is, that's my son!" and it was. He was born at 7:31 a.m. on July 31st. **7/31 at 7:31**. I should have played those numbers in the lottery. Gabe, and then two years later Paul, were both born with full heads of dark hair, which vexed Toni whose baby girls were bald until somewhere in their second years of life. I was now a father. I could only hope to become a daddy and later a dad. Such tiny, fragile, bundles of potential. I don't understand how, when experiencing this magnificent marvel of new life, can anyone dispute the existence of God.

One month later, I was being transported back to Okinawa. I had a pocket full of pictures of my new baby boy and wife. I had purchased two cassette recorders, one in my sea bag and the other one left with my wife. We would record tapes for one another and describe our days and weeks including pictures. It was awfully hard not watching my little guy grow for his first six months of life.

I was placed on guard duty the last two months on Okinawa. As a sergeant, I was placed in charge of a small guard unit that would patrol different areas of the base. There was a motor pool, a fuel depot, an armory, and various areas of the flight line that my men had to keep safe from, I'm still not sure what.

This was 1979, we were done with Vietnam. The Okinawan people were content with all the nice American money being spent on their little island. Well, we had to guard the government property from all enemies, real or perceived. It wasn't bad duty, mostly because I didn't have to walk one of these posts. I had a vehicle (sometimes a jeep; sometimes a large truck) and a driver since I wasn't allowed to drive. I made a game of it. Let's call it *let's see who I can catch sleeping*, or my personal favorite, *who can I sneak up on and scare the daylights out of?*

The motor pool and the armory were my favorites because they were great places to hide and observe while not being observed by the unsuspecting sentry. My best move was to have my driver stop a couple posts down from the motor pool. I would get out and hide for a while and continue to the next post without me in the jeep. I would creep over to the trucks being guarded and wait until the guard sat down on a truck bumper to rest a bit. In my best Marine Corps crawl, I could scoot the length of a truck without making a sound. I would then grab an ankle and listen to first a bit of a gasp then a little scream, followed by the plethora of really bad words, some of them inquiring about my sexual preferences and some anatomy terms not suitable for sensitive ears. They cooled down quickly when they first realized they were not going to die and second that their sergeant was the one who caught them resting and not the captain. Great fun! (Hey, it was Okinawa in 1979. There wasn't a lot of entertainment. I had to find my own amusement.)

I was not the kind of guy that would write someone up unless it was really bad. Like the time I had to write up my corporal for discharging his side arm (a 1911 45 cal. pistol that should not have been loaded) into my troop transport truck. The projectile entered the cab of the vehicle in question narrowly missing both my driver and me, then embedding itself into the engine of this wonderful taxpayer funded piece of equipment effectively killing it along with the corporal's chance of making sergeant.

I was due to be separated from the Corps in March of 1980. So, my stay in Okinawa was shortened. I was determined not to re-enlist. Even when my commanding officer offered me a promotion to Staff Sergeant and an appointment to the recruiter's school. I turned him down and resumed my life as a civilian and my life as a daddy. I spent eight years on active duty in the corps. I will never forget the experiences I had nor the places I had the honor to serve. There are things, rather unpleasant things, that have to do with the war in Vietnam, that I would like to forget, but can't.

Then there was the way we were treated when we returned to the country, we were told we were defending, we were not accepted. We were told not to wear the uniforms we were so proud of, but to change into civilian attire as soon as we disembarked the aircraft. This way there would be less of a chance we would be spit upon and harassed by people calling us war mongers and baby killers. There was no welcome home for us. It wasn't until 40 years later that we, as Vietnam vets, would greet each other on the street or in a store, sight in on each other's cap, or tee shirt and say, "Welcome home brother."

People who never knew us would stop and thank us for our service. Most of us don't know what to answer. I thank them for their support and move on. I am proud of my time as an active service Marine. Once a Marine, always a Marine. I am proud to have been willing to fight and die in the service of our great country.

Chapter Six: Home Again, Home Again, Jiggity Jig

When I separated from the Corps, I had to return to my place of enlistment to collect unemployment until I found a job. I had a family to support. The three of us moved in with my parents, still in Cicero. I registered for unemployment and settled in thinking about what to do next. My wife hated Cicero and the entire Chicagoland area. After only two weeks of not working, I started a search for a job. I found one working in a factory that made salad dressing and the *secret sauce* for Big Macs. I was not happy there. This was not the upwardly mobile career I had envisioned for my future, but it put a few dollars in my pocket and more importantly for me, got me out of the house. After a couple months of this, I was offered a job that paid way more money back in California. My brother-in-law worked at a metal company that was amid a labor dispute and needed people to work in the warehouse. I jumped at the chance. Maybe I could make my wife stop hating her existence. So, we packed up the car and headed back west. I had to evict the tenant that was renting our double wide trailer so we had a place to live, and we settled into our domestic tranquility once again.

Shortly after I settled in working at my new job, we bought a house a little closer to the job. We were able to sell the double wide, making a nice profit, giving us a down payment for our new dwelling. It was a small house in an older neighborhood, but it served our purpose. It was not mobile and did not shake when someone walked through it. (It took a California earthquake to get that one to shake.) I used my G.I. Bill and was able to keep up the payments, if sometimes just barely. I started taking night classes at the local community college. Again, taking advantage of my G.I. Bill, which paid for my classes and books. It also paid me a stipend that helped make ends meet, with a little extra.

This is when I learned to play the saxophone. ***Sidebar:*** To this point, I had only played the clarinet. I even entertained the idea of joining the Marine Corps Band. The band director of one of the many Marine Corps Bands, was on Okinawa while I was stationed there, and granted my request for an audition. My dad, the carpenter, made a wooden box, and mailed my clarinet to me on Okinawa. I would find a secluded spot on base and practice a few tunes and scales. I guess my audition went well, because I was offered a place in the Marine Corps Band that toured the Far East section. My commanding officer received the congratulations letter and request for transfer to the band from the band director. I was summoned to his office, where I was offered a seat. (Being offered a seat in the Commanding Officers office was either a good thing, or there could have been a death in the family.) He then proceeded to read the acceptance letter from the band director. This letter written in the formal way all military letters are written, praised my willingness to join the band. It further went on the congratulate me on being accepted. My commanding officer smiled at me and shook my hand. He had me sit down again. I was happy, this would be a nice change from the manual labor required of a young corporal in an aircraft shop. Then the other shoe dropped, or should I say Murphy hit me upside the head with a combat boot. The letter was received the day before the squadron was due to leave for the Philippines and to Vietnam. The last phrase of my acceptance letter sealed my fate. "This transfer is only to be carried out if the needs of the Corps can be satisfied by its completion." Sympathetically, my commanding officer told me that my transfer would not be in the best interest of the squadron, the Corps, or the nation. How can you argue with that? "Aye, Aye Sir!" was the only reply I could have made, without being on his list. (You know what list that is.)

Back at college, after enduring an insufferable semester of a music appreciation class which was a prerequisite, I found a loophole. I could join the band. Better, there was a jazz band I could join. The only problem was, there were no parts in the band for clarinet. When I met with the jazz band director, he offered a solution. He loaned me a baritone saxophone, and a fingering chart.

He walked me through Saxophone 101 and I joined the jazz band. This was fun! I did really well, and all the ladies think saxophone is sexy.

Then we were again with child. Great! Another child. I was incredibly happy and proud to be a daddy again. On July 23, 1981, Paul came into my life. This birth was less complicated that the previous two years earlier. The C-section was scheduled this time so I was able to schedule time off work. This time it was my in-laws who were in the waiting room with little Gabe and me. As the announcement of Paul's entry into this world came blasting over the P.A. system, I scooped up Gabe and strode toward the viewing area. Gabe was two years old and starting to talk rather well for his age. I was standing, holding Gabe up so he could see. There was a nice little old nun standing next to us. Gabe gave the nun an anatomy lesson that only a 2-year-old could. The normal head, fingers, nose, and mouth, in his little lisping pronunciation. Then he made a few other observations that confirmed to all around that he indeed had a new baby brother.

Paul, like Gabe, had a full head of dark hair. Paul's hair however, stood straight up and could not be tamed until many years later when spray starch was mistakenly used instead of hair spray. Paul, in direct contrast to his physique today, was a husky baby. Some would say round or jolly. Face it, Paul was a fat baby, with hair that stuck straight up. If I didn't know better, I would have accused Jim Henson of using my young son's likeness in the design of his Muppet Babies—not the cartoon that my granddaughter watches today, but the Muppet Babies that were puppets on the old *Muppet Show* in the 1980s.

Chapter Seven: I Am a Truck Drivin' Man and Sometimes Not...

Somewhere in the next couple years, my marriage started its descent into darkness. I lost a couple jobs (...probably due to my own fault and maybe my temper. Let's not delve into that can of worms.) and I was depressed. I didn't realize I was depressed, but I sure was not a happy camper. I decided to pursue my lifelong dream of becoming a truck driver. I investigated the ways available to me to achieve my goal and found a truck driving school not too far from home. I investigated further and with a loan from Dad, I could enroll and complete the course in four short weeks. The school would then assist the new graduates in taking the exams necessary to obtain a Class D driver's license. (This was a couple years before the classification of CDL or Commercial Driver's License, was incorporated.) I excelled in all aspects of truck driving. I could figure out a driver's logbook. I could calculate time and distances. I could even calculate miles-per-gallon of fuel. I learned how to inspect and adjust air brakes and check tires and all other aspects of a thorough pre-trip and post-trip inspection. I was ready to get behind the wheel of a behemoth of a truck and hit the open road.

Finding a job that paid a living wage was another slight bump in the road. (It felt like a good place for a bad pun.) The year was 1983, I was a newly minted, certified truck driver with absolutely zero experience. The only job I could get was as a trainee or second seat driver in a team operation. Doesn't sound too bad until you place into this equation the first seat drivers. These individuals were more than not, less than stellar in their moral compass, as well as hygiene and even sobriety. They couldn't find jobs with the larger better paying trucking companies, so they settled for the lower paying jobs that tended to look the other way when it came to complaints and brushes with the law. This was not an ideal setting for someone who really wanted to learn and get the proper experience to make a go of a trucking career.

The first trainer it was my pleasure to be attached to was a drunk. (Alcoholics go to meetings.) I was in fear for my life when he was behind the wheel. This was an 18-wheeled, 40-ton monster. We drove from Little Rock, Arkansas to New York City, New

York. He would complain about all aspects of being a truck driver. When I asked him why he didn't just quit and find other means of employment, he said, "I love the freedom of the road. There isn't a boss breathing down my neck all the time and my wife doesn't let me drink beer when I'm at home." This was when I first got scared.

The place we had to deliver our frozen cargo of vegetables was Hunts Point Market in The Bronx. This was like a third world country in America. The streets were littered with every kind of trash (human and refuse). There were abandoned cars that seemed to be used as homes. Trucks of all shapes and sizes were lined up on what looked to me to be side streets. I witnessed a pickup truck jockey itself between two 18-wheelers. Two men climbed on the hood of the pickup, cut the lock on the larger truck, and proceeded to hand boxes of frozen meat back to two more individuals in the rear of the pickup. There was a driver in the pickup and an armed guard with a pump action shotgun. This was the second time I got scared. When I expressed my horror to my first seat (let us call him Bubba, only skinnier), who told me that it happens all the time. If you get hit, just let the dispatcher know where and how much they took, and the insurance takes care of the rest. No one fights back or calls the police, and no one gets hurt. These were highly organized groups of men; there were the ones you see and then the backup ones you didn't see but were out there protecting their compadres.

I was then regaled with what was later known as *A Hunt's Point Myth.* Like most trucker stories it starts, "Now you ain't gonna believe this, but . . ." So, at this point, don't believe it, it's probably not true.

Here goes: Bubba told me like this or as close as I can remember, "There was these two good ol' boys from Georgia, and they were tired of gittin' their load ripped off goin' to the market. So, they decided they would turn the tables on the thievin' (place body part expletive here.) Before they drove the truck to the side street to get in, one of the boys got in the trailer and the other one closed the door and didn't lock it. When the thieves opened the trailer door, they were lookin' down the bore of a double barrel shotgun. The two thieves didn't panic and just stepped back onto the hood of the pickup truck. The good ol' boy in the trailer was then shot dead by one of the guys that they didn't see. The body was pushed to one side, and the thievin' commenced. That's why nobody fights them no good thieves."

After unloading our freight and getting a reload, we were on our way back west. The way our team was supposed to work was, one drove while the other tried to get some sleep in the little sleeper berth behind the driver's compartment. This seems like an equitable arrangement. There are a few flaws in this; first would require both parties to sleep in a bouncing rocking truck. (When I say bouncing, read bone rattling, knock the fillings out of your teeth, convulsive gyration that the NASA astronauts have experienced aboard an Atlas rocket.)

The second flaw is the noise in the truck. These trucks are not in the least bit quiet, adding to the cacophony generated by the powerful diesel engine is your team driver who is listening to loud music and the equally loud CB radio, so a corpse embalmed on the way to the grave couldn't sleep.

The third aforementioned flaw would require that both parties were NOT drunks. As soon as we stopped to change drivers, I was able to get a little sleep while Bubba consumed a six-pack of a certain amber beverage accompanied by a couple snorts from another bottle secreted in his toolbox. (I never saw Bubba use a tool.) After a couple of hours while Bubba was imbibing, I slept soundly. When he was sufficiently lubricated, he woke me up and would say, "It's your turn in the hot seat. Don't bounce me around and don't kill me." He would then climb into the sleeper and start snoring, loudly. I could hear the rumble of Bubba's rattling over the roar of the engine. I drove for as long as I could before my eyelids started to become very heavy.

I had to stop and get some food and coffee. When I pulled into the next truck stop, I saw that Bubba woke up. He started in on me for being a lazy, no good Yankee rookie. I ignored him and, after parking the truck, (not easy when you are no good Yankee rookie) went in to eat and refresh my still rattling bones. After a sumptuous meal, I went back out to where I parked the truck. It wasn't there. Bubba's sense of humor reared its jolly head. As I wandered around the truck stop parking lot, I tried not to let my panic rise. Did Bubba leave me here? Did someone steal the truck with Bubba drunk in the back? Then I spotted the re-parked truck backed in between two substantially larger rigs and there was Bubba, laughing his head off and holding his latest bottle. I was awake at least and I had another three hours to drive. I drove my 8-hour shift and I was exhausted. I found another truck stop and woke up Bubba. He said, "I'm a goin' in to get some vittles. I'll be out directly." It was my hope that he would give me enough time to pass out before the bone rattling started. Just as I was getting comfortable, Bubba was back. He got his food to go and sat there in the driver's seat and turned on his loud country music. Sleep once again was not in the cards for me.

We crossed through Wyoming and Utah and entered Nevada. At the first truck stop/casino we came up on, Bubba said, "I need to stop in here for a little bit. You go ahead and get some shut eye. I'll wake you when I git done." Ten hours later, I woke up without the assistance of Bubba. I was hungry, thirsty, needed a shower and aware that if we didn't get moving very soon, we would not be on time for our delivery appointment in the Sacramento area. I ate and showered. I felt a little more human than before. I filled my thermos with strong coffee. I was ready to go. Still no sign of Bubba.

I looked in every part of the truck stop. No Bubba. Then I spotted the casino across the parking lot and aimed myself at it. I found Bubba. He was sitting at a blackjack table where he had not only lost most of his money but was so drunk that I needed to enlist the aid of another patron to get Bubba back to the truck. Getting him up inside the cab was another chore that I hadn't signed up for. Good thing he was so skinny. I couldn't have hoisted a fat Bubba up and into the cab.

Now the badmouthing started again. This time his words were even less comprehensible than his normal drunken self. There were references to the parentage of the low down... (more expletives, curse words and body parts). He then went into a rant about how women shouldn't be allowed to be truck drivers. After that one, he managed to belittle not just me but all Yankees. (It seems Bubba never got the memo that the Confederates did not win that long ago war and in fact didn't exist any longer.) Then he burped loudly and passed out in the passenger seat. I was not a happy driver.

We had to be in Sacramento, California and I was the only driver capable of actually driving. This was a little over 500 miles. We had 10 hours to get there. Easy you say. There is a little problem there. Mountains. There are a lot of mountains in the Western United States. Nevada has some pretty steep ones that slow a big rig down to walking speed. The worst mountain pass on Interstate 80 is Donner Pass, so named after the Donner party who were stranded in a particularly nasty snowstorm back in the winter of 1846 and 1847 and ended up being legendary for their culinary tastes. I was a rookie; I had no experience with such a driving feat. This took skill which I hadn't achieved yet.

I had to give it my best. I recalled all I knew about mountain driving that I was taught in truck driving school. I stopped and inspected my tires and thumped them with a small bat to see if any tires were flat. ***Note:*** Flat or under inflated tires mounted on dual rims cannot be seen as flat or under inflated with the naked eye. Thumping them on the tread produces a distinct sound when tire pressure is sufficient. If you ever see a truck driver thumping his or her steering tires, he or she is a rookie. A flat tire on the steer axle would be obvious and the truck would not be drivable. I then took my trusty 9/16th wrench and adjusted the brakes. I could do this; I was ready.

I entered the highway and said a little prayer that Bubba and I wouldn't become a messy statistic. The first part wasn't so bad. What's all the fuss about? Now the climbing started. The truck engine strained and I did my best to downshift without grinding gears. I didn't do too well in this arena. Bubba woke up. Now I not only have to concentrate on my driving, but I had to put up with the driving critique of a foul mouthed, Southern good ol' boy who couldn't see to walk much less drive.

Downhill was scarier than Bubba's driving. There are little gravel roads leading uphill called truck escape ramps. These are not something that anyone ever wants to have to use. This was explained in detail, even illustrated with a video of a test truck being captured by the loose gravel on the escape ramp. (This would have been an E ticket at Disneyland.) The other deterrent from using the escape ramp was the financial one. There was a hefty fine and a towing fee and the fee to repair the ramp for the next trucker who failed to slow his or her truck sufficiently to safely navigate this most dreaded slice of interstate highway.

When we finally made it to Sacramento, my shoulders were stiff and my hands were curled into claws. Bubba was still drunk from the day before, so I called for instructions and delivered the load. When I called dispatch asking for a different partner, I was told that I could not, and would have to finish a 6-month period before I was allowed to change partners. I told them that I would not be working for their company any longer and phoned my wife, who came and picked me up.

There was silence all the way home. It seems someone was not as on board with my dream to be a truck driver as before I started classes. It was a very long ride home. I started looking for work as soon as I got home. There were not many in Southern California at this point. I tried and looked and went on interviews but had no luck. I sold my motorcycle to make a mortgage payment. I did odd jobs to keep food on the table. I finally found another trucking job that had me again driving in the second seat with a lunatic. At least he wasn't a drunk. I hadn't gotten much better at sleeping in a moving truck, but I was paying my dues and collecting experience points.

After a few months, I was given my own truck and made first seat. Now I had the responsibility of showing the ropes to a newly minted driver. This was more like the blind leading the blind. I had only had my license for eight months, but I again did my best. I went through five, second seat rookies in as many months. Then I found one who worked out and we became friends. We were actually making money.

It was hard work driving as many miles as we could handle. We both dreamed of a time when we could land a local job and spend time with our families. We were both veterans and talked long hours of our experiences in the war. When my marriage slipped farther down into its final inevitable oblivion, I decided that moving back to the Chicagoland area would be my next step. My parents took me in, and I again started looking for gainful employment. Landing a job with UPS was a fantastic opportunity that I hoped would last and that I could build into a career. It was not to be. I was hired in November and the job lasted until the day before Christmas when I was laid off until needed again.

I tried my hand at an auto body shop for a while but didn't possess the skill to make any real money. I had my CDL, so I found a driving job that didn't require me to share the truck with anyone. Things were looking up. I found driving solo was where I fit in. I was also able to take as many trips to the West Coast as I could handle. This meant I could see my boys and that was great. I missed them and now that my parents had moved to California after my dad retired, I had a place to stay when I was in town. I was able to bring toys for my guys and pay child support. I enjoyed the freedom of the road and relished my solitude.

Little Paul did not talk early like his brother did. Paul had Gabe to do all the talking for him so why should he talk at all? Paul also had a medical problem that started early in his life. He has asthma. He was watched over with the hope that he would outgrow the malady as I did when I was a child. On Christmas when he was 3-and-a-half, he had a bad attack. We were visiting my sister Karen and her husband Rich who lived in Whittier, California. Paul was playing with his cousins when he started wheezing, and gasping for breath. I only panicked for a moment, as any parent would do. I snatched him up and was out the door. My other brother-in-law Dale, was a Los Angeles County Sheriff Deputy, so he drove. He drove at remarkably high speed, and we were at the closest emergency room just before we left. (Ok, maybe not quite that fast, but pretty darn quick.) Paul was inspected, prodded, and poked. He was given oxygen and steroids. At this point, pumped full of stimulants, Paul started talking. He got out all the words that were building up in his little brain for three years and they all came out in a flood. Paul hasn't stopped talking to this day. He just needed a jump start.

Chapter Eight: I Have Two Boys and That's It!

I met wife number two back in Berwyn. She was going through her own marital problems, and I was an easy ear and shoulder to cry on. We would enjoy each other's company when I rolled into town, and love blossomed. I decided to look for a job in Chicago. Maybe a local trucking job that would keep me close to home. (Home being a little apartment in Cicero; what they called a studio garden apartment.) I accepted a position with a company that manufactured point-of-purchase displays. I now used my military training as an aircraft metalsmith to obtain a spot in the metal model shop. This was fun and I formed a few new friendships. I learned a lot about blueprint reading and fabricating the first run models of the displays. These models were then disassembled, and the various parts were set up in large noisy machines to be churned out by factory workers that didn't speak English as their first language. I was making a fair wage and settled into a happy existence.

I was working in the shop one morning. The only two people there that morning were my supervisor and me. It was January 28, 1986. We had the radio on and just going about our tasks for the day. I'll never forget what happened next. The radio announcer broke into the music we were listening to with a breaking news bulletin. The space shuttle Challenger had blown up 73 seconds after it blasted off into a clear Florida sky. I remember staring at the radio, and then locking eyes with my boss. Neither of us could move nor speak. The boss reached for the radio dial and turned it to a local news station. The same horrific description was flooding our speakers and our minds. The Challenger had been in the news due to the fact the first teacher was to be up in space. All seven crew members were killed that day. The nation and the world were saddened by this devastating news. My thoughts and prayers are still with those brave men and women.

Second wife and I purchased a house from my paternal grandmother. Grandma lived alone in Stickney, Illinois. My Uncle Pete lived with her after his own marital demise until he passed on. Grandma insisted on living in her house. Dad and I would do what we could to help her out, all the time trying to convince her to move in with my parents who were planning their own move to California. Dad and I would do repairs and paint. We would be rewarded with some of Grandma's fantastic Italian meals and of course Grandma's smiles and hugs. Grandma was close to 90 and we found any excuse to visit and check up on her.

The winters were hard on Grandma. It was hard for her to get to daily Mass, and with Dad and I both working, and mom teaching school, there was no one to drive her. Her one luxury, as she called it, was to pay the extra money to heat her house so she was comfortable. (The Finnish people have a word for a house with such heat. It's called a sauna.) When we visited, we would wear layers that could be peeled off. No one ever complained. Grandma deserved to be comfortable. She earned that right. In one of these winters, Grandma didn't want to bother anyone, so she donned her heaviest coat and scarf, got her galoshes on over her shoes, and ventured out. She used no cane, nor walker, and even pulled one of those two wheeled carts behind her through the icy, snow packed sidewalks. Grandma walked down to *Da Jewels* (Jewel grocery store) four blocks away. When her shopping was completed, she began her walk home. Grandma slipped and fell on some ice that had accumulated on the path leading to the sidewalk from the store. She sat there for no one knows how long, until another little old lady helped her to her feet. Blessings were bestowed, and Grandma continued her trek back to the comfort of home. No one knew what had happened, and no one found out until several days later, on a Sunday, Grandma announced that she was ready to move in with my parents. When asked what caused this change of heart, the saga of her fall and the angel who helped her up came out in a torrent of words and tears. We were stunned that this would happen as much as the fact that Grandma was scared enough to show emotion is this way.

The house was offered for rent to us at a less than market rate. It was small, but manageable. Dad and I built a shed in the back yard for storage. Since grandpa never drove, there wasn't any reason to have a garage, so none was ever built. I built a bedroom in the basement and purchased bunk beds from the local military surplus store. Picked up a few other items at garage sales and had a place for Gabe and Paul. In the summers, the boys would be transported via airplane to stay with me for their school vacation. We had great times; camping, going to stock car races, and their favorite, demolition derbies. I was always sad when summer ended, and I had to ship them back.

After a couple years at the display company, I accepted a better paying position at a company that fabricated ice machines. These were made of stainless steel and were used commercially at such places as fast food restaurants as well as stadiums and finer eating establishments that required a large quantity of ice. I sold my grandparents' house and bought one closer to work. Wife two found a good job near home too, so money was pretty good. She had a daughter, who being several years older than the boys, was a built-in babysitter throughout the summer months. There was a lot of work to be done on this latest house. The previous owner, thinking himself a handyman, attempted remodeling himself. On the surface the house looked pretty good. When digging deeper, the flaws came to light. Wife two and I ended up remodeling every room in the house. In one bedroom and in the living room, we had to remove the wall board. In a few places along the outside walls, we had to remove rotted wood and replace it with new.

The kitchen needed to be re-plumbed, and a new floor was needed because of the leaking sink that wasn't addressed before Mr. handyman installed his version of a new floor. Peel and stick tile that could be cut with kitchen scissors was his idea of adequate.

The bathroom was a total disaster. This room also had to be reduced to studs before I could make it usable. (Good thing we belonged to a local gym, so we could shower until the bathroom could be made safe.) Mr. handyman had built a storage bin above the tub. This massive structure was strong enough to hold a couple motorcycle engines. It was strong enough to store the lost gold of the Incas. It also blocked what little light emanated from the one light fixture on the ceiling, and blocked half of the window, making it impossible to clean. The number of nails haplessly hammered into this monstrosity could have been used to build a small subdivision of modest single-family dwellings. It took longer to demolish this disaster in DYI construction than it took me to install new drywall in the bathroom. A new tub was installed. A new sink was installed. The wiring was scary. I enlisted the help of a friend who was an electrician's apprentice to help me out here. (The thought of burning down this house did flicker into my consciousness a few times, but I resisted the urge.) Paint and trim plus some new light fixtures and we had a functioning bathroom. It looked good too if I do say so myself.

This was the time a decision was made. We both had children and neither of us wanted any more. Birth control pills have side effects and wife two was taken off the medication by her doctor. There were still options for us. The first and least painful was a visit to our local drug store to purchase the little raincoats that prevented both more offspring and the spread of disease. This method was used for the short-term solution. The second solution was surgery. This would be a long-term permanent key to yummy sounds coming from the bedroom. But, which one of us would go under the knife? Do we flip a coin? Do we cut a deck of cards? Maybe a foot race? None of the above. The decision was made, I was to go under (gulp) the knife. I was informed that since she had been taking the pill and suffered the side effects from said pill, it was only fair that I would have the procedure. Further encouragement came when she flat out said, "If you ever intend to enjoy any more yummy sounds in our bedroom, or anywhere else in the world, YOU WILL HAVE THE OPERATION!" How could I argue with that kind of logic? I made the appointment and set a date on a Friday that coincided with a three-day weekend. I was told what to do after I got home. This consisted of lying in a large supply of ice and a couple days' worth of G-rated Disney movies.

The day came way faster than any time in my life, but here it was. YIKES! I drove to the hospital with wife two in the passenger seat trying to soothe my less than enthused self. We parked and went inside. I was ushered into a small operating theater and told to disrobe and put on the gown and lie on the metal table and wait. This time was spent reflecting, praying, and just plain fear. Here come two small Asian nurses. (At least there were no nuns involved.) One started attaching probes and other wires to my head, chest, arm, and fingers. The other one was getting the other end of me ready. This is when she exclaimed, "You didn't shave. I guess I'll have to do it for you." I never saw anything in the reading material given to me that said anything about manscaping. I never saw the logic in having a sharp object down there. I then reassured myself that she was a professional who did this sort of thing every day. She set about her task. I was not reassured. The nurse watching the monitor then said, "Your blood pressure has spiked a bit, are we a little nervous?" There was a lady with a razor scraping hair from the boys, of course I was nervous!

Now the drugs were administered. This was better. All my anxiety seemed to melt away. The doctor came in and greeted me in soothing tones. I have no idea what he said, but I felt surprisingly good, for now. There was a needle stabbed into each of the boys. For several seconds, (that seemed like an hour-and-a-half!) the drugs were not enough. I'm sure my blood pressure again spiked. When this excruciating pain subsided, I was able to relax my grip on the sides of the metal table. (I think my handprints are crimped into that table to this day.) Now the fun part. Waiting the prescribed time, the doctor started his work. More pain seeped its way through the anesthetic and other drugs, and it felt like being kicked or run into headfirst by a 2-year-old. Not a pleasant sensation at all. I was prescribed oral pain medication, an ice pack, and another pamphlet instructing me what to and what not to do in the next few days.

I waddled into the house and eased myself into the recliner that would be the place I would reside for the next three days. It was nice to be waited on, and the drugs were nice, but there was a fair amount of discomfort that lingered. I watched the Disney movies and kept an ice pack in the affected area. After three days, I was able to leave my chair and return to work. I wasn't ready to compete in a marathon, but I could walk without wincing. I stopped taking the drugs the night before, so there was still a bit of discomfort. It wasn't anything I couldn't handle. The period until I was to see the doctor again and be able to share yummy sounds with wife two, unlike the speed with which time flowed before the dreaded operation, moved slow, much like the big rig climbing an extremely steep mountain.

The day came when I showed up for my appointment. I was shepherded into an examination room where I was to wait for the doctor. Instead, one of the small Asian nurses came in with a small cup. Thrusting this cup into my hand she then instructed me to fill the cup in the manner that the nuns and priests along with other adults from my youth said not to do in fear of my ocular health. I'm not sure what my blood pressure was doing, but I could feel my face brightening to a vivid scarlet. The nurse then opened a drawer and indicated a stack of reading material, (I am pretty sure no one did any reading in here) and she promptly left the room.

After making my deposit, I pressed the button that would summon the nurse. She trundled in and collected the sample I had provided. I was still in a state of facial blush attributed to my ever-growing state of embarrassment. Fifteen minutes later, in strode the doctor. He mumbled his greeting as he sternly poured over my chart. He then started speaking in doctor speak, numbers and terms that only trained professionals could understand. When he looked up from the chart at my bewildered face, he told me everything I wanted to hear in one phrase that I'm sure he had uttered many times with the same smile. The doctor said, "Well, Ed, you are now re-zoned recreational." He further informed me that my yummy sounds in the bedroom could commence once again. Woo hoo! Let the fun begin. For another year, things went rather well. Then things went sideways agains

Chapter Nine: Murphy's Law: Whatever Can Go Wrong Will!

Heeeeeeere's Murphy! My boss was not fulfilling his obligations at work. He was let go. My hours were drastically cut and the money was getting tight. (I had been working an average of 50 hours a week that was reduced to 40 hours a week in a snap.) My reaction was less than conducive to further employment at this company. (Did I mention that I had a temper in those days?) A term that has been bandied about is *flew off the handle.* Another would be *went off the deep end.* The fact is, I threw a tantrum, saying some things I couldn't take back. Not my finest hour. Looking for another job while trying to keep my depression sort of in check wasn't working too well.

I tried a couple promising endeavors, but none worked out more than a couple weeks. What next you ask? Truck driving. I signed on with a company out of Hudson, Wisconsin and hit the road again. I was again in a solo operation and soon proved myself a pretty good employee. I was awarded a very prestigious route that turned out to be a lucrative endeavor indeed. I was one of two drivers assigned to an exclusive custom cabinet manufacturer in Minnesota. The client would ship the cabinets to the Southwest United States. This was great for me. I could see my boys on a regular basis. I could visit my parents and sisters too. Plus, the return trips almost always came back to Chicago, where I was able to spend time at home. It was at this point that I purchased my first truck.

I ordered a brand-new Freightliner with a double bunk, a Caterpillar engine, and a 13-speed transmission. This not being a company truck, it didn't have a governor on the engine. In other words, it was fast. I had a chrome wing installed on the top of the cab and had my name, and the name of the company I was now an owner-operator for, painted on the doors. I had pinstriping artfully painted on to highlight the lines of my new beauty. I came up with a name for this first truck and borrowing the font from *Star Trek TNG,* I had *The Starship Freightliner* hand painted on each side of my sleeper berth. I was out there making money. Solitude was a good remedy for my depression. (This in fact turned out to be PTSD, not diagnosed until much later.)

I incorporated and started looking to expand my little trucking empire. With the help of a small inheritance coming on the heels of my paternal grandmother's demise, I was able to purchase a second truck. I had a driver lined up to be my first employee. He qualified through the company who performed a background check, a physical, and the essential drug test. This new driver was to take over my *Starship* and I was going to pilot my brand-new Freightliner. This new truck was even larger than the first. It had not only a double lower bunk, but a second bunk that would be stowed away above the first one. You could stand up and walk around in this truck. Such luxury. I couldn't wait to take delivery. Again, Murphy came to kick me in my tail section.

While traveling from Minnesota to Chicago with a locked and sealed trailer loaded with cut paper stacked high on pallets, I made a mistake that cost me a lot of time and money. As I left a truck stop in Wisconsin, I took the tight clover leaf entrance to the highway a little too briskly. I was on my way home after negotiating the purchase of my new truck and hiring my first new employee. I was tired and my mind was on home and the new truck, not on my driving.

I miscalculated the clover leaf and tipped over. The paper slid off the pallets and assisted in upsetting the entire rig. (Insert expletive here; maybe more than one expletive.) At least I wasn't hurt; shaken, but not stirred. I had been wearing my seat belt and my TV landed in my lap. Everything was tossed around and the truck was badly bent. The cargo was lost and the trailer was totaled. As I was crawling out of my windshield, a good Samaritan said, "Hey buddy, give me any drugs you have in there and I'll get rid of them for you." I didn't have any drugs. I never took drugs that were not prescribed by a reputable doctor. Caffeine and nicotine were my vices.

The *Starship* was towed to a local repair shop. I was driven over to pick up my belongings, and wife two drove up to pick me up.

She was shaken too, and we both chain smoked all the way home. The next day I realized that I was a little more stirred than shaken, with bumps and bruises, but my pride suffered the most damage. I spent the next few days on the phone with insurance adjusters, the safety team from the company, the repair shop that was going to rebuild my baby, and my new employee. Let's call him Bubba two.

Bubba two was all ready to start driving, but I had just bent his truck. I drove my car up to the dealer in Minnesota and took delivery of my new truck. I sighed and gave the keys to Bubba two who would be piloting my new baby until the *Starship* was out of space dock. I had four long weeks to wait, but at least I had a truck in the game that produced a nice revenue stream.

Bubba two was a good driver and was happy with his wage. I paid him five cents a mile more than the company did. After carefully driving my new truck for four weeks, he secured a load returning to Chicago, where he picked me up and headed to the repair shop in Wisconsin. My *Starship* was repaired, re-painted and ready to go. I instructed Bubba two where to go in the Twin Cities to have the sides repainted and even let him have his name hand painted on the door. I was in my new baby and I was happy again.

I continued to service the cabinet company and Bubba two ran wherever the dispatchers sent him. After about six months or so, Bubba two contacted me and told me that he had a friend who was a company driver for the same company that we were signed on to and was looking for an owner-operator to drive for. Once again, Piane Trucking, Inc. acquired another new truck. I now had two employees, and three trucks. In a short time, my little trucking company was making enough money to be two months ahead on truck payments.

I kept two $100 bills in my wallet and I told my two drivers that if either one or both surpassed me in mileage for a month, I would surrender the money to the winner or winners. I never had to pay up.

Things were looking up for my financial status. Wife two was working, and we were way ahead in truck payments. We even put some money in a savings account. Until then a hard scratched out existence with little or no financial safety net was our lot in life. We bought a very small house in Romeoville, Illinois, but now the walls were starting to close in on me. Another house was purchased in Joliet, Illinois. This was a newly built house in a new subdivision. It had that new house smell. There was plenty of room for our little family, and a place for the boys when they came to visit.

I found a young couple with one child to rent our Romeoville house and started furnishing the new one. Not bad for a guy who couldn't read until late in high school. (I did get my high school equivalency or GED while in the Marine Corps.)

If I would have stopped there, I might have been fine. I bought two more trucks and hired two more drivers. Piane Trucking was reaching for the sky. This is the point in time when I found out, (the hard way of course) that it was nearly impossible to run a trucking company from behind the wheel of a truck. Especially in the days before the widespread use of cell phones or laptop computers that could be used at any truck stop with a Wi-Fi connection. Not to mention mobile banking and other computer stuff that we take for granted today.

Drivers started flaking on me. Loads were late and I was fined. Trucks were breaking down and I was charged for repairs. The company threatened to terminate my lease if things didn't start getting better. Then I had my first two drivers, Bubba two and Friend of Bubba two, quit. I had to get myself up to Minnesota, retrieve my trucks, and hire two more drivers. This proved more difficult than before because of tighter regulations in hiring CDL drivers. Thank your U.S. federal government's Department of Transportation (DOT).

Finally, I sought and found another company to lease my trucks onto. Some of the managers from my first company jumped ship and started a new company in Eagan, Minnesota and I followed. I had four drivers for my four trucks and things were on an even keel again. I started looking for someone to drive my truck and found a husband-and-wife team that passed all the tests and new regulations. I now had six employees and a rental property. What could possibly go wrong? Murphy's ugly law. That's what could go wrong.

I received a phone call in the middle of the night. It was the hubby from my team. He was calling from a truck stop in Indiana, it was winter, and he was cold and only had a light sweater on. The phone booth was outside. All of this was spoken very fast through chattering teeth. (Yes, we used phone booths with phones mounted in place, and yes, you had to feed coins into the device to make it work. I get it, I'm old. GET OFF MY LAWN!) He then informed me that the wife of the team was in a foul mood. They had a quarrel and when hubby went into the truck stop to get some coffee, wife absconded with the truck. The load was heading toward Texas where the team resided. Wife was headed home. I forwarded hubby enough funds to allow him to travel to Texas on a bus. (This money came out of his paycheck.) I purchased an airline ticket to the town where the load of freight was headed. I showed up at the receiving customer an hour before my truck was due. Wife of the team backed into the dock and saw me standing there. "I quit!" was all she said in greeting. I ended up picking up the next load, which was already booked by dispatch, and drove out to California, all while trying to maintain order in my company and my marriage.

"The only difference between a puppy and a truck driver is that the puppy stops whining after six months." It seemed my drivers got annoyed with dispatchers, police officers, me, wife two, and other truck drivers. Not to mention, anyone driving a four-wheeler, retirees driving RVs, politicians on either side of the isle, the weather, and of course lady truck drivers. I may have left some groups out, but you get the drift. I was constantly trying to hire new Bubbas, because Bubbas were looking for greener pastures faster than I could hire them. I finally seated five Bubbas in five trucks. I was treading water, but at least the sharks were gone. Breakdowns were few, and I was making truck payments and payroll.

I was bored not driving or having a job to go to every day. So, I dove off into the deep end. I leased a gas station and repair shop in Joliet. Then went into business with wife two's sister and brother-in-law. What was I thinking????? How could I have been talked into such an endeavor??? (Must have been the same kind of persuasion that had me under the knife a few years back.) I had *too many sticks in the fire*, as one of my Bubbas used to say. *Burning the candle at both ends* was another witticism bandied about, along with *running around like a chicken with its head chopped off.*

I worked long hours at the gas station; I was trying to finish rooms in the basement of my house, so my boys could have a place to stay when they came to visit. Hiring Bubbas and keeping the trucking company busy also took up considerable time. Dealing with my sister-in-law daily was not conducive to good mental health. (Remember, I was not yet diagnosed with PTSD.) I was frazzled, and depression was starting to tighten its grip on my entire being. It seemed that no matter how hard I tried or how hard I worked, I couldn't seem to move forward. I kept slipping farther behind. Financial trouble began to worsen. I am no accountant, but I knew something wasn't right. It seems wife two and her sister were not being fiscally conservative enough to break even not to mention make a profit at the gas station. I started smoking again. (I had quit smoking eight years before and was doing well until now. Wife two never quit and that was not easy to live with.) I also couldn't sleep despite the long hours and stress.

Enter Murphy, stage right. On a sunny Monday morning in September, I received a call from one of my Bubbas. He said, "Ed, my fuel card ain't working and I can't get ta-holt of the dispatch." I told him to stand by and I would contact dispatch and page him. (Yes, we used pagers way back then. Don't make me tell you about my lawn again.) As I hung up the phone, another Bubba called with the same complaint. I gave him the same instructions and started dialing the dispatch number. No answer. I was starting to feel a twinge of anxiety forming in the back of my brain. Before I could dial the private number of the safety department, my phone rang again. A third Bubba, no fuel card, no dispatch. The twinge became larger and a little more penetrating.

I dialed the safety department's number with no results. I called the company president's private live and then his mobile phone. (Only rich guys had mobile phones back then.) No one was answering. Now the twinge turned into a panic. What do I do now? I want to run away and hide. I can't though and I know it. I call a dispatcher friend of mine who was still working for the first company that the second company broke off from. It was divulged to me in hushed tones that the second company just closed its doors. The president and a few of his managers had run off with the assets. My friend knew this because members of the local and state police had come to the first company's offices on Saturday morning looking for leads on the whereabouts of second company officials.

Over a hundred company drivers, and over 50 owner-operators were stranded all over the country. I had two trucks in the Chicagoland area. Three trucks far away; one in Nevada, one in Utah, and one down in Mississippi. This may be the very point in time that my bald spot started, and my beard started to gray. I contacted my Bubbas. The one in Utah was instructed to deliver the load to the customer there in Utah and drop the trailer in the customer's lot. It wasn't the customer's fault the bunch of, (insert body parts here) and felons went belly up. The Bubba in Nevada was told to drop the trailer and, if he could, sell the tires on said trailer and purchase fuel for the trip home. Mississippi Bubba had a full tank of fuel, so I told him to abandon the trailer and bobtail up to Chicago, and we'll regroup and see what we can come up with.

At this point, the company owed me over $15,000 for services rendered and another $5,000 in unpaid insurance and truck payments that they were supposed to be making for me under our contractual agreement. I also had to wire money to two of my Bubbas to get them back. (Selling tires was not working.) Grand total loss, $22,500!

I was now scrambling to find a new company to lease onto. I was frantic. I finally found a company that would take four of my trucks. My fifth Bubba found a company that he wanted to pull for and I consented. Good going Bubba! Now here comes another curve ball. The new company was happy to sign on four trucks and drivers, however one of my Bubbas was not able to pass the required background check. Well three out of four wasn't too bad. This gave me an idea. I would drive my biggest truck and earn some needed money. (I obviously didn't learn the part about trying to run a trucking company from behind the wheel of a truck.) I reminded myself that we needed the money, and I was qualified to drive. The underlying reason just might have had a lot more to do with my marriage slowly falling apart, and my dealings with my business partner in-laws. I found my way to run away.

I was out there running the wheels off my truck. I accepted every load offered. I learned ways around keeping just one logbook, and how to skirt weigh stations. With the aid of a CB radio and a radar detector, I never got a speeding ticket.

My father would ride along with me now and then. He loved going to the cabinet company when I was still hauling for them. Dad was a carpenter for many years, and now retired, enjoyed looking around the factory and the smell of the freshly milled hardwoods. We enjoyed conversation and listening to books on tape together while I did the driving. (Yes, books on tape, no CDs yet and no MP3s, cassette tapes. (OFF THE LAWN!)

I accepted a very lucrative run that started with a full load of frozen strawberries picked up in Port Hueneme, California. The load was then transported all the way across the country to Hollywood, Florida. There the load of frozen berries was removed from the trailer. This same trailer was then reloaded at the same dock. I now had a full load of frozen juice bars destined for the children of all ages in Los Angeles, California. It was a grueling trip with only stops to grab food and fuel, and little sleep. The 18 hours it took to unload and reload was spent catching up on sleep and visiting my cousin who lived in the area. This run paid well and, being the dead of a particularly cold winter, I was happy to be in the south. Dad accompanied me on only one of these grueling round trips. He told me he was not built for such excursions. We contented ourselves with my visits to California and Mom and Dad's visits to Chicago.

The gas station back home was not doing well. Sister-in-law was drawing more salary than was being taken in. The mechanic we hired was doing more side work than work for the station. Two months later, I received the news that everyone involved with the gas station, except for me who had invested all the capital for the venture, decided to close the station. There were bills such as gas in the ground, oil that was delivered, utility bills, insurance premiums, and our accountant who needed to be paid. Now it came to light that two of my latest trucks had payment well overdue. In the words of Good Ol' Charlie Brown, "Good Grief!" What did the in-laws care? It was my money that vanished. They had no skin in the game. (Or as one of the Bubbas would have put it. No dawg in that hunt.) Top it all off with wife two siding with her sister against me, and I was done. I moved out of the house. For a moment, I contemplated keeping the rental house in Romeoville and moving into it myself, but my attorney advised me to sell the house, and use whatever profit I received to pay down the substantial debt I was drowning in. So, I got myself a little apartment. I became my own Bubba, and just drove.

When one of my trucks was taken to the Freightliner shop in town, I was informed that Freightliner Financial repossessed that truck and asked the whereabouts of the other truck that was also in the rears of payments. Ok, I thought, three trucks are easier to deal with than five. Maybe this could work. I had a team in one truck who hailed from an Eastern European country. For a couple months, they did a great job and money was flowing in slowly but at least coming in. At the end of the aforementioned nasty winter, I got a message from dispatch that the Eastern European Bubbas had vanished without a trace. They had taken their belongings after collecting their paychecks and simply vanished. I drove to the company offices and truck yard to do some business and see if I could get some help hiring another Bubba. I opened the door to the abandoned truck, and the smell was overwhelming. The Bubbas (not only body parts go here, but questions about parentage and sexual preferences involving eastern European Bubbas and farm animals) had totally trashed my truck.

I was devastated. I know I was not the neatest driver when I was on long hauls with little time to clean up, but this was a disgrace. Cigarette burns, empty soda cans, food wrappers, and half eaten food were everywhere. A couple of gallon jugs that had been used as urinals completed the party. There was even a five-gallon bucket half filled with plastic bags of poop. I removed much of this trash and waist into a dumpster, including the two mattresses. I called the company that cleaned and detailed trucks for the company drivers and had them do the rest of the cleaning work. Now I made one of my better decisions concerning my little trucking company. I drove this truck right over to the local Freightliner store and put the truck in question up for sale.

I offered the last Bubba standing, to help him get financing so he could buy the *Starship* from me. It worked and I was down to one truck to worry about and me being out on the road with way lower blood pressure. It was at this point that I met who would become wife three.

She was working in the office next to the trucking company that insured the company drivers and company trucks. They offered reasonable rates for owner-operators. Wife three was going through a divorce, and so was I. (There is a pattern here.) We dated when I was home, and things were going well. Turns out we were both getting over our second marriages. (Something about doing something the same way and wanting a different outcome, seems exactly what I was doing here.) Figuring that wife to be three was working in the trucking industry, this could work out. Well, it did, for a while.

Wife to be three, was a girlfriend at this point. She shared an apartment close by, with a girlfriend. Then Murphy came to visit her. She lost her job. She also had a less than stellar divorce attorney, who took his fee out of the pitifully small settlement she received from her ex. She was broke, and jobless. I offered her my apartment, after all we made some yummy sounds when I was home. I wasn't home a lot anyway, so she moved in.

She moved in with two cats. I never owned a cat. I knew next to nothing about cats. I was educated in the finer points of care and feeding of cats. Why do we bother naming cats? They never come when you call them. Cats don't come running when they hear you come into the house no matter how long you've been gone. Cats could care less about food carefully picked out for them. Cats go crazy in the middle of the night, running and trying to climb the walls while making a totally sinful wailing. I must say, it is fun watching the little buggers chase a laser pointer though. I do not currently, nor do I ever plan to be owned by a cat ever again.

My solitary trucking life was going well. I took all the loads I could handle, most to the West Coast, and things were going well. Wife to be three found herself a job working for a trucking company and was very understanding of the trucking lifestyle. I was able to visit my family who were all out west by now. The apartment we were sharing was being converted into a condo, so when the change came, I purchased my condo and life rolled along swimmingly.

Wife to be three became wife three. I was home a little more often and decided to look for a local position. I leased myself and my truck, (the big double bunker that I had named *Ed's Jazz Wagon*. This was before the rainbow symbolizes what it does today. I had a large, stylized saxophone with neon notes on a rainbow musical staff coming out.) onto a national company that was hiring local owner-operators to run the intermodal rail lines that were growing in the Chicagoland area.

Now I was home every night, so I started playing my sax again. I answered an ad in the area paper aimed at musical groups and bands, and after auditioning, I was accepted. The band had a core rhythm section, drums, guitar, bass, and a lead singer. This was the early '90s and swing music had returned, making quite the big splash. I was the first sax player to enter the scene. I had a baritone and a tenor sax, and I practiced as much as I could squeeze into my schedule. The second sax player was introduced, and he could really play the tenor. He also played the alto sax. We were starting to gel as a band, but something was missing. When the tenor man introduced us to trombone man and trumpet man, things really started sounding great. Not only did the trumpet man play a mean horn, but he also arranged music for the horn section. This was starting to be fun.

The two young men who started the band, booked a couple of gigs at a few of their favorite watering holes, and they drew nice crowds of their friends. I figured I'd try my hand at booking our band. I, with the help of my sister Karen, made up business cards, and Karen designed a logo for the band. I made up a small tidy press kit which included a professionally taken photo and a bio of the members, and a list of songs the band performed. A CD was added much later. I visited clubs that featured live music and had dance floors for all the swing dancers. Then it struck me. I will try this newfangled Internet and see what I can find. Maybe find more gigs.

I was and still am far from any kind of a tech whiz. That being admitted right up front, I will divulge the depth of my ineptness with computers. Being in a swing band that played swing music, I typed in the search bar, *swing clubs.* Lord have mercy, that was an enormous mistake as you can just imagine. I got plenty of responses. I even got a lot of unwanted pictures of people in various stages of undress, most with eyes blacked out. This was not the results I wished for. These people were all crazy. They requested pictures of me and wife three. They further requested pictures of us without clothing. They told me in very explicit ways, what they wanted me to do with their spouses. Or what they wanted their spouses to do to me. This is when I was made aware of my error. I promptly closed my AOL account and started the email account I still have to this day. (Old dogs and new tricks.)

The band had fun and played a lot of gigs until the bar owners realized something crucial to their livelihood. Swing dancers were not buying booze. They wanted bottled water and soft drinks. These people were dancing and getting exercise. This was the death toll for swing music in local bars. The band went their separate ways and we tried to keep in touch, but failed. We still talk on the phone now and then to catch up, but don't get together anymore. It was lots of fun while it lasted. I finally sold my *Jazz Wagon* and accepted a job with a trucking company to be their maintenance manager. On the same day, wife three also started her new job at the same trucking company. Let the games begin!

This company was in a western suburb of Chicago. We both worked long hours and commuted together. I was issued a cell phone and a pager and was expected to be on call 24/7 to assist our growing number of Bubbas that broke down all over the country at all hours of the day and night. I was used to middle of the night calls from my own Bubbas, so this was not too different. I had been all over the country, so I knew where to send these company employees to have their company equipment repaired.

This amazed friends and family when at a holiday dinner party, I would answer my phone and instruct the driver on the other line. I would give him directions from where he was to the nearest truck stop or repair facility. A short while later, I would get another call from the repair shop and give them the authorization. The third call would be from the shop manager requesting payment, at which time I would issue a Com-Check number from the little notepad I always carried. I felt very important, and I felt needed. It was a good feeling even if such calls would come in the midst of making yummy sounds. Kind of spiced things up a might.

After several months, the company lost its driver recruiter. I found myself taking phone calls from potential new drivers and expounding the virtues of this particular trucking company. The owner overheard one of these conversations, and I was then given a crash course in hiring Bubbas in the way it was done by the company and how they expected it to be done. I was now a recruiter; I was also still covering the maintenance. You would think maybe I would have received an increase in salary. You would be wrong.

I now had to place ads in trucking magazines and newspapers all over the country. I had to keep up with the Bubbas breaking down all over the country. I received phone calls and had to sell the company as a great place to work. I had the prospective Bubba orally fill out a phone application, at which time I would say, "Very glad to talk with you, and if you'll call me back in two days, I'll have an answer on your application." It was at this point that

I enlisted the help of one of the other office workers to vet the prospective driver. (More times than not, this turned out to be wife three.)

If the last few companies verified the information given over the phone and there weren't any objections from the boss, when the Bubba called back, he was issued a bus ticket voucher. When he arrived, he was placed in a local motel and given a packet of paperwork to read and fill out. Even food vouchers were provided.

Arriving at the terminal the next morning, he was immediately taken to the clinic for a drug test and physical. The conference room was converted into a classroom, and one-by-one, the different department heads would come in for a brief instructional talk. I covered maintenance and safety. I gave classes on how we wanted our logbooks filled out. I gave classes on hauling hazardous materials. I instructed the newbies on how to secure their loads. I even gave classes in defensive driving.

On the second day, we got the results of the drug test. It still amazes me that when someone knows that there will be a drug test administered, they would study for this test by ingesting, snorting, or smoking controlled substances. This was not an isolated incident; it happened at least once a month. These Bubbas were shown the door and had to find their own way home. The ones who passed not only the drug test, but successfully jumped through all the hoops, crossed the t's, and dotted the i's were taken out to meet their trucks.

The company trucks were not the newest on the road, but after being checked out by me and our mechanics, then cleaned and detailed by a local mobile cleaning company, they were ready to roll. There was only one Bubba who, when seeing his new ride, decided he didn't want it and requested another truck. This didn't sit well with the general manager, (a rude, vulgar, narcissist, and all-in-all real bully. The bane of my existence), who told the man, "You can drive this truck or walk home to whatever trailer park or log cabin in the backwoods you crawled here from." To his credit, the driver picked up his bag and silently started walking away. The general manager bully's face fell. He was going to have to tell the owner why, after spending three days training, a bus ticket, and the cost of a physical and drug test, this highly qualified driver with tons of verified experience, was walking out. Back peddling, the bully then said, "What I meant was, that you have to drive this one for now. We'll be taking delivery on a few new trucks in just one month and you will be able to drive one of those if you will take this one for the time being." (He never apologized for the trailer park or backwoods comment.) That driver, the last I heard, was still with the company and has proven to be an excellent employee. (Don't you just love a happy ending, at least to that driver's story.)

After working for this company for a couple years, it was announced that the company was moving to Romeoville. (This is the part when I was regretting selling the rental Romeoville house.) A building was purchased with the accompanying five-acre lot for the trucks and trailers. Plans were made for the upgrade of several loading docks. There was now to be a maintenance shop including five tractor bays and a larger bay to accommodate 53' trailers. Also planned for was a parts room. The work was done; the date for the move was set. This was going to be a lot of work, but we were going to hit the big time. Weeks were spent packing up offices, with all the files boxed up for transport. Computers were carefully bubble wrapped and placed in large crates. The trailers that were not out on the road, were enlisted for use and loaded up. There were three trailers loaded, the only problem was that we only had one tractor in town. So, what do you think happened next? Yup, Bully Boy, had me make three trips.

I had to drive the backroads, because the wonderful trailers that were being used were not road worthy. One had only five tires (normally having eight.) Another had not passed DOT inspection and had no brakes. The third had only four tires and no working lights. Wife three was drafted to follow me. (I guess to pick up any parts that might fall off on the way.) This cross-town illegal transport took all day, and I was beat. Home and bed for me. Tomorrow we were starting fresh. And in the immortal words of any movie character setting up a plot twist, "What could go wrong?"

I showed up at our new digs bright and early the next morning. I was slightly surprised that wife three and I were the only ones in the parking lot. Bully boy was always the first to arrive. 20 minutes later, the owner came racing in, followed by a salesman and a dispatcher. I didn't know him well, but I could tell that the owner was rather upset. He unlocked the front door and bounded into his new corner office, slamming the door behind him. None of us knew what was happening. This was a day that was supposed to be a happy one, even if we knew we all had a lot of work to accomplish so the wheels could keep rolling.

The four of us were summoned into the office. We timidly obeyed. With quizzical looks, and more than a little trepidation, we entered and were offered seats. We were then told that our general manager (AKA Bully Boy) called the owner on his cell phone and informed him that he would not be joining us in our new office space, effectively leaving us all holding the bag. I was all at once shocked and elated. The bully was out of my hair. Shocked at the fact that the rest of us would have to take up the slack. The salesman, a close personal friend of the owner, was made General Manager. I was made Fleet Manager. Essentially putting me in charge of hiring drivers and all of truck maintenance. Wife three was put in charge of safety. It was at this point that we found out that the renovations to the building were only partially complete and that the maintenance shop was only a shell with garage doors only partially installed. There was a lot more work to do than any of us were counting on.

The shop was mine. (At least what there was of it thus far.) The first thing I had to do was get a phone hooked up to my office. I of course had a company mobile phone, but that wasn't to be used for non-driver related calls. I acquired the rolodex from the office and started calling vendors to help get the shop finished. There were no tools, there were no parts, there wasn't even any oil. I had the garage doors wired up properly and they were in working order.

I found out that to perform oil changes we had to have a containment pit, constructed around the waist oil tank. We didn't have an air compressor, so one had to be found that was large enough to accommodate tractor trailer work. I needed to get a parts list together including an inventory of nuts and bolts needed by mechanics daily to keep trucks and trailers roadworthy. An extensive inventory of the various lights, involving bulbs, fixtures, and sealed beams used on several different vehicles. Mechanics had to be hired. Diesel mechanics, as well as at least one trailer mechanic, would have to be found. Ads in local papers were placed. A containment pit was constructed. An oil tank, as well as a waste oil tank, were delivered and installed. Parts were delivered and stacked in the parts' room. We were getting close to having a real working maintenance shop.

Two mechanics were vetted and hired. A trailer mechanic was also hired, and things were looking up. I spent long hours from Monday to Friday, we only worked half days on Saturday. After our first in-house routine maintenance complete with oil change and fluid top off was completed, the owner called our new general manager and me into his office. Hearty handshakes were administered and we were asked to sit. The boss started to extend his gratitude for all the great work that we had accomplished since the move. We beamed with the praise; this was nice. Now I let my mind wander a little and the concept of an increase in pay lurked there. This thought was soon squashed by the next statement. Owner said, "Well, things are a little slow right now, and the departure of our former General Manager cost a great deal of money to set straight." He then went on to promise financial increases when things started improving. Oh well, I guess Murphy comes in many forms.

I waited, put in my long hours in the office, and was on call 24/7, all the while trying to keep the shop running smoothly. I even proposed to the owner that it might be a good idea to invest in an inventory of tires along with the tools to change tires in our own shop. This was met with enthusiasm, but not more money in my pay envelope.

I hired a tire man and taught him how to work our new tire machines. With all the hours I was spending at work, and still being a salaried manager, I realized that the mechanics I was supervising were making more than I was. I mustered up my courage and made an appointment to see the boss. The General Manager was in the office when I was let in. I sat in the same chair and listened to the same praise I heard last time. This time I was told that due to the extra people we had to hire in our new tire bay plus the extra inventory of tires, that it would be impossible to raise my salary at this time. The owner then said, "If you will just wait another year or so, I'm sure things will get better." Then he strode out of the building and got into his new Mercedes and drove off to play 18 holes of golf at his country club. I looked at the General Manager. My mouth was still open wide with my eyes unblinking. I had no words. I walked out and headed for home, where I got my resume together and started surfing the Internet for a new job. Do you blame me?

I interviewed in Indianapolis, for a job in Chicago. After a second interview, this time in Chicago, I was given the nod. I would start my new job in two weeks. I went out and purchased a *new-to-me* car. I would have a rather long commute and my little Fiat was not going to cut it. I happily gave my notice and started getting my office a little more orderly for whomever my replacement might be.

My new commute was slow and tedious, but I was making more money, a lot more. Even better, when I left the old company, wife three stayed on. When she was given more responsibility, she was given my old salary. We were making more money now and decided to sell the condo and buy a house. This would make my commute a little longer, but hers would be next to nothing. I was now maintenance manager for the Chicago terminal of a large trucking company.

Things were not easy; the mechanics resented me for taking the place of their friend who held the position before me. This was my first encounter with a union shop too. Discipline could not be achieved the same way that I learned in the Marine Corps. My dealings with all my previous employees and Bubbas didn't help much either. I sought advice from my superiors and other friends, and was able to make some headway. There was even a spark of respect forming in the shops.

Chapter Ten: September 11, 2001

The next disaster hit and hit hard. The world would never be the same.

This was a clear sunny day in Chicago as we went about our workday tasks. I was in my office having a conversation with my parts manager. The radio was on, but neither of us was paying attention to it. Then the news director came on and the radio gave out a shrill tone. This, of course, was September 11th, 2001. At the first announcement of a plane crashing into the World Trade Center, we were thinking of maybe a small private aircraft that had an accident. I remember thinking, the poor pilot, and hoping no one else got hurt.

Then the next alarm trilled, and the announcer painted a much bleaker picture of what they were calling a terrorist attack. When the plane that crashed into the Twin Towers was described as a large jet passenger airline, I was in a slight state of shock. I called the rest of my team in, and we all huddled around the radio. The next thing we heard was that another jet airliner crashed into the second tower. We couldn't believe what we were hearing. When the reports came in about a plane crashing into the Pentagon, and then one crashing into a field in Pennsylvania, we were convinced that these were the first shots in a new world war.

We found a television set and switched it on just in time to witness the first of the towers crumbling to earth. After a short time, the second tower also came down. The pictures of people covered with thick choking dirt came unsteadily to the small black and white TV screen. We were all shocked, stunned, flabbergasted, deeply saddened, scared, and very, very angry.

From the parking lot, we could see the John Handcock building as well as the Sears Tower. Going out to look at Chicago's skyline was the new normal that day as well as in the next few days. We were convinced that Chicago would be the next target of these cowardly monsters that attacked our country. As the death toll rose, our hearts sank lower into grief for the victims, their families, our country, and the world. There were a lot of flags flown at half-staff. Everywhere you looked Old Glory could be seen on flagpoles, in windows, and from most car antennas. I called my family and expressed gratitude that we were all spared from this tragedy. We thanked God for our safety, and that of our family.

We were angry and wanted to fight, but we had no idea who to wage war against. Was it our old enemy Russia? Could it be a newer enemy like Iraq? For days there was speculation, but no clear facts. There were hundreds of able-bodied young men streaming into the recruiting offices of every branch of the armed forces. Even some salty old vets, myself included, called, and were told, "Stay at home gramps, send your sons and daughters." I was only 48; I was fit, but I saw their point. Old guys like me don't follow orders as well as we used to. We tend to question authority, and that would not be any good in the service. My son Gabe, on the other hand, walked into the Marine Corps recruiting office and raised his hand, signed up on September 10, 2001. (What timing!) He spent several tours in the Middle East and is still in the Corps. Eighteen years later, Gabe is now a highly decorated Master Sergeant. He and his wife gave me two wonderful grandchildren. Still, the world will never be the same.

The trucking industry was hit extremely hard, as well as a good portion of the rest of the economy. Companies were going out of business. Other companies were *downsizing*. (This was a new term being tossed around that meant the same as *tightening your belt.*) Consolidation of company assets was how the memo was stated when I received it that next January. They were merging the three terminals in the Chicago area into the one central Chicago terminal. This also meant a reduction in personnel. I was the junior maintenance manager and not belonging to the union, I was downsized.

Oh joy. I seemed to be out of work. There were also not any companies looking for an out of work maintenance manager. There were not any jobs for driver recruiters either. I couldn't even find a job as a truck driver. This was not good. Unemployment at least kept food on the table, and with wife three still employed, we were able to stay ahead of bills. Life was not fun. I started downsizing too. I sold my camper trailer; I sold a small boat and motor. I did a lot of online job searches. It wasn't until that fall that I finally found a trucking job.

After being idle for so long, I was ready to leave my stress-filled life of cleaning kitty litter and trying to fill my days with doing something meaningful. I was ready to hit the open road once again in a big rig. For one year I drove a company truck, doing my best to make some much-needed money. This new company recognized the value of motivating their drivers with a carrot instead of a stick. The dispatchers didn't yell at drivers and the key word was safety.

A conversation might go something like: "Hello Mr. Bubba. Can you tell me why your load was delivered two days late?" and if the answer was, "I'm so sorry, but the weather was not cooperating and there was rain, snow, sleet, fog, it was dark at night, and the sun was in my eyes during the day, and I had to rest a lot for safety's sake." If the driver invoked the *S word*, there was no further action taken.

I was once again content in my solitude. Books on tape became books on CD, and I could check them out of my local library for free. I had a CB radio in the truck but was seldom on it. I carried a small refrigerator, a microwave, and a coffee pot. I would take leftovers from home and even better, leftovers from my family in California. I spent less time in truck stops eating overpriced, fat laden food that was always covered with thick gravy.

The new rules concerning logbooks worked fine for me. Drivers could be on duty for 14 hours in a day, 12 hours driving, and were then required to take 10 hours off duty. I would drive my 12 hours (Maybe a little longer.) and was then able to stop and park for the night. At a truck stop, I would fuel up the truck and get a nice hot shower. (You would think truck stop showers would be nasty, but they were kept and maintained surprisingly well. The truck stop maintenance crew cleaned thoroughly before the next driver was let in.) After my shower, I would either make a meal out in my truck, or sometimes grab a bite inside the restaurant that most truck stops had. Then eight hours of sleep. The thrumming of the diesel engines all around, and the little vibrations, helped me to drift off and recharge my batteries for the next day. In the morning, I had a chance to have breakfast, coffee, check my logbook, and hit the road again.

In this period, my blood pressure was down from the previous few years in the office and shop. I asked for as many west coast trips as the dispatchers could find for me. I was now checking up on my parents. My kids had friends and their own lives to live. They usually made time to see me, and we would have some fun in southern California. My parents were getting older, and I worried about them. Getting the opportunity to spend some time with them was priceless.

So, things are going nicely. Wife three is content with her job. We were able to talk every day due to the newest cell phone technology. What do you think I did then? No not that. Not that either. Give up? I BOUGHT A TRUCK. I know, the whole doing the same thing and expecting a different result. Sanity is overrated. Life is way more interesting when you are just a little crazy.

I bought this truck from the company I was employed at as a company driver. The improvements in trucking technology and comfort were, in my humble opinion, fantastic. This new truck was a Volvo, a RED Volvo. It had a bigger, more powerful engine than my last trucks (even the famed *Starship Freightliner*, or *Ed's Jazz Wagon*). The air ride suspension was surprisingly smooth for such a large vehicle. So with comfort and power, I set out to, once again, seek my fortune. I again set up a corporation with the crazy idea that I could build up a company with lots of trucks and lots of Bubbas to drive my beautiful trucks, while I pursued hobbies and raked in the money. After all, wife three was in the trucking industry. She would help, right? I was older and wiser now, right? What could go wrong? (Sounds like a broken record, doesn't it?) Stay tuned for more plot twists and ensuing wackiness.

Chapter Eleven: Good Morning Mr. Murphy

My big red truck and I were happily rolling down the interstate highway of life. (Sounds poetic, kind of like Mongo in *Blazing Saddles.*) The money was better than that of a company driver and there was a little more respect afforded owner-operators.

(Maybe it was fear of crazy people who would buy trucks.) Things were pretty nice for a change.

Then from out of nowhere came a message that was something like this: "Control here, this is a general call out for a Mr. Murphy, Mr. Murphy please respond as soon as you get a moment. Thank you that is all." After a few moments. "Control this is Murphy standing by for orders." Control continues, "Good morning Mr. Murphy, are you available to administer one of your laws in the next week?" Murphy responds, "Let me consult my schedule." We hear paper shuffling. Murph calls out: "Stella, what's on the calendar next week, and don't schedule anything on Saturday, I have a 7:30 tee time at the club." Stella in a Brooklyn accent, (Hear: Annie Potts in the original *Ghostbusters*.) Says, "Monday morning is wide open, from 2:00 a.m. to 5:00 a.m., Mister 'M'. Should I pencil them in?" "Yes Stella, I'll get back to you with the details doll. You're a peach." Stella blushes. (She is secretly in love with the boss, but that is another story.) "Control, Murphy here, I'm free this Monday morning, what's the job?" "Mr. Murphy I just noticed that Ed Piane is solvent and happy. Can you help us out here?" Murphy scratches his chin. "Let's see, we wrecked his truck by turning it over, then ruined his trucking company by having another company go under. (That was a twofer.) We managed to ruin another marriage and have him lose another company. What do you think of going back to a nice truck wreck?" Elation enters control's voice. "Splendid my boy. We'll look for the results on Monday then. Have a nice weekend and hit them down the middle." (That's a golf reference in case you were wondering.) "Thanks control. Talk with you Monday." Then said, "Stella, we have some plans to make and some timing to set up. Could you stay a little late tonight?" All a flutter now, Stella responds in her best husky, breathy voice, "Anything you need Mr. 'M', anything." So, they plot and plan, and set up timetables. With a triumphant, evil little grin, Murph announces, "This is a great plan, can't wait for Monday. Let's call it a night Stella. I bet your cats are missing you. See you Monday morning." Once again, dejectedly, Stella says, "Goodnight Mr. 'M.' Have a nice weekend." And under her breath utters, "My darling." Let's face it folks, Stella doesn't have a snowball's chance in the hot place down there, with Mr. 'M'. Golf and really messing up people's lives is the only thing he cares about.

The weekend was uneventful. I drove through Utah, a little of Arizona, and Nevada. I stopped on the California border to get the truck washed and fueled. I grabbed a bite to eat and settled into my comfy sleeper and got my eight hours of sleep.

This is a federally mandated logbook regulation that will get you a nice fine for violation of these rules in most states. In California, the fine at that time was a staggering amount, because they could. This is also why we would have our trucks washed before entering the *Golden State.* Dirty trucks were often pulled over and inspected vigorously, and (back in the day), inspectors would find something wrong with the equipment, and a healthy fine would follow.

There was a notorious set of inspection scales (For some reason we had a slang for these weigh stations all over the country, *Chicken Coops.*) in California, (I won't say exactly where.) that had an atrocious reputation for this practice. An inspector would indicate for a dirty truck, (sometimes a clean one if he was bored) to pull into the inspection bay and take his logbook into the main office. While the unsuspecting driver was sweating the review of his logbook, the equipment inspector, (We had a slang term for these guys too, *Creeper Cops.*) started his work. He would check lights and air lines and fan belts. If he found nothing wrong, he would advance to the brake inspection, where he would produce a 9/16th wrench and un-adjust the brakes on the tractor, showing a direct violation resulting in a fine. This is not where this ends.

The Creeper Cop would then take the driver aside and give him a business card of someone who would come out and professionally adjust all the brakes on the truck and the state fine would be averted, and the driver could pay the mechanic and not have any points on his license. The driver was stuck. He or she would have to fork out money either way. Most would opt for the local mechanic, who was later, as the story unfolded, identified as the brother-in-law of the Creeper Cop. Money changed hands with a wink and a nod. After the federal DOT got wind of this lucrative scam, a Creeper Cop was fired, fined, and incarcerated. The shady mechanic lost his business and was also fined. Back to the story.

Midnight Monday morning. My logbook is up to date, I had just completed eight hours of sleep. My truck was shiny and clean. I head for LA, maybe I could beat the heavier rush hour traffic. (There is no time when there is no traffic in LA.)

I have a heavy load in my trailer, but I've driven these roads before. In the early morning, the cars and trucks are moving smoothly as we negotiate the hills and curves on our way to La Land. The speed limit was being maintained as the procession of steel and rubber surged westward.

Enter Murphy. I don't know if he pushes a button, invokes an ancient incantation, or simply waves his hand, but things start going squirrelly fast. As I take an easy right-hand curve, I notice a lack of overhead lights ahead. The road is also sloping downward, not too steep, but not flat. I am traveling at the prescribed 55 mph.

As I take the curve, seemingly out of nowhere, a car materializes sideways in my lane. It has no lights and it isn't moving. With no room to swerve due to the other cars and trucks on either side of me, I stood on my brakes and gripped the steering wheel. I t-boned the car, and not just any little plastic car; this was a full-sized Crown Victoria. The momentum of my truck and the approximately 30-ton load behind it pushed this mammoth car 30 feet sideways down the highway when we came to rest in the same center lane I was occupying from the start. I was in shock. The

Crown Vic was folded around the front bumper of the Volvo. The Crown Vic was also painted in the familiar yellow of a taxicab.

My shaking fingers found my cell phone and I dialed 911. I informed the operator of the accident. When she asked if anyone was hurt, I swallowed and said, "I am fine, but I can't see any movement in the car." I told her that I would get out and look. As I was opening my driver's door to check things out, she shouted, "No! Do not leave your vehicle. Wait for the Highway Patrol."

As I closed my door, a large SUV came alongside me, slowed to rubber neck, and was promptly pulverized by a big rig, who was traveling too fast and tried to pass on the left of the commotion in the center lane. Now I was doubly quaking in my driver's seat. Were there people riding in that taxicab? Were any of them alive, or maimed, or dead? For the next 15 minutes, I prayed, and chain smoked.

When the first officer came on the scene, he blocked off all westbound traffic and set up a perimeter of cones and flares. He came to my driver's side door and the first thing he asked for was my logbook. Seeing it was in order, he motioned me to get out of my truck. We grabbed flashlights and started toward the unrecognizable hulk of twisted yellow steel.

Shining our lights into the twisted wreckage of this former vehicle, there was no blood, no mangled bodies, no one at all. I could once again draw breath. There were other accidents all around us, and there were a few injuries, but no fatalities. The 5-hour freeway shut down was covered on the news that evening, but all in all, we were all pretty lucky. The abandoned Crown Vic had just been purchased at auction by a man who gave it to his daughter as a 21st birthday gift. The former taxi had stopped running and the young lady pulled it over to the center freeway divider. She and her friend, being a little bit inebriated, simply exited the car, and made their way to the right shoulder of the road and walked to the nearest gas station.

This young lady failed to place the car in PARK, nor did she engage the parking brake. As the traffic on this stretch of freeway increased, the vibrations caused the car to start rolling. Murphy's timing was spot on, but no one was seriously hurt, just twisted metal. Most of it was able to be repaired. My truck was severely damaged, and it took over a month to get it road worthy again. I lost some revenue, but the company loaned me a truck, so the loss was minimal. As I mentioned earlier, I did a lot of praying while sitting in my battered truck waiting to see what fate had in store for me. Yes, Murphy caused a lot of chaos that day, but God trumps Murphy.

After an interminable seven weeks of driving an older, less comfortable company truck, I got my baby back. The new red paint gleamed. The front tires were new, and with the new alignment, it was a sweet, smooth ride. Everything worked like when it came out of the factory. Before the crash, my left headlight was cracked and water had seeped in, making the light a bit faint. It would have cost me around $250.00 to buy the part and a lot of labor to repair it. Now I had two brand new headlights*, in your face Murphy.* I spent time refitting the sleeper to make it even more to my liking. I found a place for golf clubs, and my tenor saxophone. I worked hard miles and relaxed when I could. This went on for another two years. I was keeping up with bills and saving a few dollars for a rainy day.

WW II
VETERAN

Chapter Twelve: Becoming BAPA

My son Gabe was married to his high school sweetheart. Gabe joined the Marine Corps on September 10, 2001. Proud papa, that's me! When the second Iraq war started, I started to worry. I knew Gabe would have to go answer the needs of his country. Gabe's wife, LeAnne was pregnant with their first child. She was in California close to her family and well along in her confinement. (There is that ancient term for being preggers again.)

The USA was on the brink of invading Saddam Hussein's land. Gabe was to be in the first wave entering Iraq from Kuwait. More prayers. I had been through that sort of thing a long time ago. I was anxious, and downright scared. I now knew what my parents went through when I was in harm's way. I didn't get a lot of sleep because I was too busy watching CNN. As the world held its breath, waiting to see what the *Shock and Awe* produced.

Trucks sat idle as freight shipments were put on hold. I was in Chicago, so at least I didn't get stuck out in some truck stop sitting with all the armchair quarterbacks, very opinionated Bubbas, who ALMOST joined the military. These Bubbas all had very convincing tales to explain why they didn't join. I endured these Bubbas when the first Gulf war was going on 10 years before. I suffered in silence at home with full media coverage blasting on the TVs well into the night.

I then received a phone call that changed my life again. I was officially a grandfather! Jordyn Linn was born April 8th. Mother and daughter were healthy and happy. My dad was the one who got the opportunity to call me. Now I was asked if I knew how to contact Gabe. I started to tell my dad what the proper procedure was and who to call. Then he told me that I should be the one to do that. This was great! I not only had great news to relay, but in the process, I would be able to talk with Gabe and find out how the war was going. I contacted the Red Cross. There were several hoops for me to jump through, and I patiently did my jumping.

When a nice lady called me back later that day, she sounded rather weary, and not at all happy to talk with me. When I gave her my information and Gabe's information, and then the request I was making, her demeanor changed. I could hear her voice brighten. She informed me that so far since the war started, she had the unpleasant duty of letting service men and women know about the death of a loved one. This was the first happy news she had come across in a very long time. Little Jordyn was making a lot of people she never knew or would know very happy indeed.

The local media in California found out about our new little angel and swooped in on the hospital where LeAnne was not ready for visitors. Her room looked like a florist blew up inside. There were balloons and banners, stuffed animals, cards and baskets of baby things and fruit. Our baby Jordyn was the first child born whose daddy was overseas in the thick of things in the Middle East.

I had advised Gabe when he entered the Corps, that it might be advantageous for him to maybe go into the Air Wing of the Marine Corps as I had done. I was told that he wanted to be in communications and be attached to an infantry unit. I explained that every aircraft that the Marine Corps flew, had a large amount of very sophisticated electronics and communication gear on board. I was overruled; not the first time my wisdom was not taken by my offspring.

When Gabe finally got the message from the Red Cross, he asked one of the embedded reporters if he could borrow his *sat* phone. I got the call. (In the middle of the night of course.) It was a very clear connection and Gabe was elated to hear of the birth of his new baby girl. I was then rewarded with the best sentence ever uttered to a parent. Gabe said, "I think I should have listened to you Dad. I should have tried for the Air Wing. Those guys are sitting back in Kuwait in air-conditioned hangers and I'm out here slogging along, carrying this heavy radio." I was overjoyed. My words did penetrate. I was not just talking for talking sake. You parents of older children know what I'm talking about. When you hear your own words coming out of your child's mouth, the sensation cannot be adequately described with mere words.

When Gabe came home after his first deployment, he was stationed in North Carolina. Now I was able to look for loads to the East Coast, and the West Coast. I did a lot of long-distance driving in those days. I got to watch little Jordyn grow from infant to toddler, and then travel out to the other end of the country to visit my parents and sisters. Paul was living in Chicago at this point, so if I was lucky, I could catch up with him and share dinner in the city. Paul was working several jobs at the time.

I would spend time at home with wife three also, but there seemed to be something lacking. There was a distance growing. So, not knowing about the old Saint Edward thing, and not being the greatest communicator in the world, I did nothing. I chalked it up to my being gone so much and started looking at alternative career opportunities. I still had my up-to-date resume circulating to be checked out by any intelligent employer out there looking for a man of my caliber.

The very next spring, one of the aforementioned intelligent employers contacted me via email. We corresponded and talked over the phone. I was brought in for an interview with the higher ups in the company including the owner. We had a very nice and expensive lunch, and I was offered a position as recruiting and retention manager. Benefits, including paid vacation, 401K, and medical and dental for wife three and me. Salary was good and steady. (When driving a truck, one never knows exactly how much money is coming in from week-to-week.) I was home every night, and only worked five days a week. It took me from June, when I came off the road, to October, to realize that my third marriage was on the rocks.

I wasn't working long hours and had weekends off. I worked around the house and even did a fair amount of the cooking. (And not just on the grill.) This was also the time that I was in another jazz/blues band called *The Sound and the Fury*. I also sang in the church choir and joined the American Legion. We had friends over for small dinner parties, we went out to listen to music.

Chapter Thirteen: Alone Again, Naturally

When the band played, wife three would show up but would leave early. I figured she had seen us play before, so I couldn't blame her for not wanting to stay for every show. In the middle of October, we hosted a Chili Tasting party. We had a house full of friends and family. Paul even trekked out from the city. It was a genuinely nice party with plenty to eat and drink. The guys in the band even drove out and some of them lived down near the Indiana border. Some of the chili offerings were a bit overwhelming in the hot pepper department, and wife three's sister made a chili without meat.

Everyone seemed to have a great time. Sunday, we cleaned up and nursed little hangovers. (I'm getting too old for this.) Monday, I went into work and things seemed rather normal. I had a dinner meeting in Elgin on Tuesday that was over in record time, so I was home earlier than expected. Wife three wasn't home.

I fed the dog and cats and sat down to watch some TV. Wife three came in about 9:00 p.m. The four words that always mean there is trouble brewing is when she says, "We have to talk." If your spouse ever comes to you and says, "We have to talk," pour yourself a stiff drink, sit down in your favorite chair and listen. Well at least pretend to listen, while calculating whether you want to try to keep the house or not, and other things like, which car you'll keep, which stuff in the house will go with you. Try to keep your cool, sip your drink, keep a blank expression on your face. When you do listen to her, you will be educated on all your many faults, and everything you may have done wrong in the past, however many years you've been married, and some things from a past life, along with some stuff she dreamed you did wrong.

Sometimes these *dream wrongs* can cause rude awakenings in the middle of your own dream with the statement, "Oh, how could you?" (Hear Laura Petrie, from the old *Dick Van Dyke Show.*)

When I started listening, after calculating about how much this was going to cost me while thinking about the lyrics to a Ray Stevens song that has the phrase, *I'm gonna find me a woman I can't stand and buy her a house,* I was informed by wife three that someone had turned her head and she had been making yummy sounds with this head turner since just before I got my new job. I wish I had been notified of this when first her head had been turned. I would have stayed on the road. I may have had the chance to pursue my solitude and maybe find someone to make some yummy sounds with me. This at least explained why she seemed a little distant and aloof, her head was turned, everyone knows you can't function properly with a turned head.

This was to be an amicable divorce. I made an appointment for the two of us to see our lawyer friend. We had just seen him at our chili party. We met at his office and walked in together. We were offered comfy chairs and the lawyer made small talk, expressing his gratitude for his invitation to our little soiree indicating how much he enjoyed himself. When he asked what he could do for us and wife three gave him the answer, he burst out laughing. When he looked at my face and realized she wasn't kidding, there was a pregnant pause.

A lawyer who was rendered speechless; that was one for the record books. He thought we needed advice on buying a piece of property or maybe a new car. We were given a couple options to consider. He was not allowed, by law, to represent both of us and the one not represented by him would have to show up at court. I graciously offered his services to wife three and told him that we could do lunch after the proceedings. Also, with the money I would be paying him, it would be his treat.

I found a two-bedroom apartment 10 minutes from work. December first, I moved in. Wife three and I shared our house in separate bedrooms. It seemed to be an extremely long November that year. I negotiated for some furniture from the house, to include some pots and pans, but no plates or silverware. With the help of two old friends, I managed to acquire enough furniture to adequately make my new apartment homey. I furnished the kitchen from Walmart and bought a bed from the local mattress store. (Can't swing a dead cat without hitting a mattress store these days.) I was already a member of a chain gym establishment, so I did spend a lot of time there. My commute was an easy 10 minutes.

I was still not a merry man. I was betrayed and deeply wounded by wife three. This is not something that can be easily shaken off, no matter how amicable the separation and divorce appears. Add in the yet to be diagnosed PTSD, frankly, I was a mess.

At work, my formerly jovial personality had faltered. I was less engaging and moped around in a total funk. I also didn't tell anyone at work about my divorce. I thought I was just being stoic and strong, when in fact I was slipping into another bout of depression. When called in the office and confronted with my attitude, my words came like a torrent of all the feelings that I had bottled up inside for the past two months. All the betrayal, the lies, all my feelings of rage, and despair spewed forth from my soul.

My immediate supervisor was a lady a little younger than I was. She was kind and matronly. Her husband also worked at the same company, in a different location. She sat there, slack jawed, gaping at me, now and then dabbing at her eyes with a tissue. If it was sympathy I was seeking, I came to the right place. She *there, there'd* me. She uttered rather unkind epithets aimed toward wife three. (I did not object to this.) I was offered a few days off to get my head together. (Without pay of course.) I declined this last part because the bills from my move and some heretofore unknown credit card bills incurred by wife three on my credit line. All I asked is that she keep this matter private. I went back to my desk and tried getting back to work.

In the next few days, I mellowed out slightly and I was even invited to join the office crowd in their weekly Friday night gathering at a close by watering hole. These were mostly young people and almost exclusively single. When I entered the establishment, I was greeted warmly, and to my chagrin sympathetically. Seems that my supervisor was a good listener, except for the part where I asked her to keep my current status private. Everyone knew. I was more than a little embarrassed. I was being patronized and consoled by well-meaning kids. Several young women threw their arms around me and expressed their sympathy. (Okay, that wasn't the worst thing that could happen. I just had to tell someone about that part.)

With more drinking, more consoling went on. I was regaled with youthful betrayal, and how cheating exes could all shrivel up and die. (Or at least a certain part of the offender's anatomy.) None of these youngsters had ever been married. The betrayal and cheating were all a part of dating. Wasn't it? I was eventually rescued by a slightly older woman (still younger than me), whom I was aware of but had never talked with. She had been married and been betrayed by a philandering husband. At least we had a common point of interest. We chatted until it was time to call it a night. I received hugs from all in attendance and headed for home.

Monday morning rolled around and I showed up at work ready to face the day. My matronly co-worker again called me into her office and instructed me to close and lock the door. Office gossip is faster than a warp drive starship. She asked me if I had a nice time Friday night. (It now occurs to me that my invitation was somehow orchestrated by the person in whose office I now shared.) She then said, "Oh I know you wanted to keep things a secret, but I thought you needed to get out and enjoy a nice night out." (Now hear Herb Tarlic's wife from *WKRP* or more recently, the mom from *That '70s Show*.) "A little birdie told me that you and divorced lady in the office (we'll call her DL because Bimbo isn't polite), were getting rather chummy." I hadn't thought we were any chummier than the other social butterflies and co-workers in attendance, but I kept silent. I was then notified that there was a no dating co-workers' policy in place, and if I was intending to pursue a relationship with DL, that we needed to keep it a secret or we could both loose our jobs. Secret?!!? In this place?!!? Now that's funny. I'd be willing to bet that this conversation would be whispered across the office floor before I could make it back to my desk.

During the next conversation I had with boss lady, she bombarded me with all the gossip that was fit to repeat, about DL. This sounded like catty mudslinging, but I sat and listened. DL was the reason the no dating of co-workers was put in place. DL had extensive plastic surgery in almost all areas of her body. DL used to be immensely fat and had her stomach stapled and her sitter-downer tucked and rolled. She tried getting her hooks into every man, young, old, married or not. I was seen to be a potential meal ticket or sugar daddy. This was even funnier than the previous paragraph. I guess at least my current financial status wasn't common knowledge. I told boss lady that while flattered, but I was not interested in DL. Nor was I interested in any of the lovely young ladies in the office. I was currently not pursuing any relationship. I hadn't recovered from the last one.

I was then told that my car had been witnessed parked in the parking structure of DL's apartment complex. This was news to me, and it was shortly verified that DL and her son lived in the same complex that I did, only in the next building down. This communication and spy network would have made the cold war CIA proud. I was innocent of the charge of making yummy sounds with a co-worker, but the seeds of suspicion were sown. I was still invited out on Friday nights after work, but rarely accepted. This was too much drama for my taste.

Chapter Fourteen: In Your Face, Murphy

On a cold, icy Saturday morning, I drove to Romeoville to retrieve some personal belongings that I had forgotten about, and drop off some things that I took by mistake. Divorce was still a month away, but the separation was going well and amicably. I had an errand to run that took me to Joliet. As earlier noted, it was very cold and very icy. I was stopped at a red light when I felt a jolt in the rear of my car. Looking back, I could detect the grill of a minivan filling my rear window. I exited my car and strolled to the rear. The minivan slid down the small hill and abruptly encountered a stopped vehicle. My car was not damaged in the least and the minivan had only a small dent in the front bumper. The driver, however, was a jittery, stammering hot mess. She was to become wife four, Nancy. (I can use her name because she said it was okay.) I tried to console her, telling her it was nothing. Her car had just tapped mine. Her bumper hit the tow hitch on the rear of my Pontiac. She was starting to break down. I suggested we pull into the IHOP parking lot and go in, out of this cold. She agreed, and we entered the restaurant and sat in a booth. I ordered coffee and she had tea. We talked regaling each other with tales of our recent separations and pending divorces. We exchanged phone numbers and made promises to stay in touch. We talked on the phone just about every day.

Nancy likes to tease when I tell this story to new acquaintances. She says, "I had to date him, I didn't want to get sued." To which I reply, "You should have aimed at a guy with a more expensive car." Then we both laugh and smooch. Telling each other, "I Love You." Old people are so cute sometimes.

When Nancy moved into her aunt's house in Lockport, I offered to help. I was told I could come to her new house, but under no circumstances was I to accompany her or any of her friends, who were also helping, to her old house. Her ex was there, and she was worried that we would get into a fight. I respected her wishes and didn't move from the house.

I met Nancy's brother and a few friends. I felt judgmental eyes all over my person. After getting to know Nancy, I was confident that I was a step up on the food chain from her soon to be ex. We spent more and more time together that winter. There were lots of yummy sounds coming from us. Nancy is so sweet; we became exceptionally good friends. We were falling in love.

My divorce was finalized first. February 14th, yes, Valentine's Day, (my lawyer friend has a sense of humor) my papers crossed the judge's bench and once again I was a free man. Later in that same month, Nancy was emancipated from her marriage shackles. Our relationship blossomed into the spring. We were happy. Friends would tell me that they hadn't seen Nancy smiling in a very long time. That made me happier, and my chest swelled with the satisfaction that I could make a positive difference in the life of someone I love.

I was in the batter's box. I looked into the steely eyes of the pitcher 60 feet and six inches away. He was kneading the ball in his glove behind his back. His front foot came off the ground as he kicked and fired a 90-mph curveball just off the plate. As I swung at this offering, I heard the ump call, "Strike!" As I glanced back at the mound, the pitcher had his back to me, and his name became visible. Murphy had thrown me a curve ball and I swung for the fences.

On Good Friday, I was called into the big boss's office where I was once again being downsized. I had been with the company for a little over a year. I was the junior member of my recruiting and retention team. I was being let go. Oh great. What do I do now? Well shoot, think Ed, you need a job and right now. Being the former recruiter, I was aware of a job I hadn't been able to fill in the company that involved a big rig, a required CDL, and a dedicated run. I requested the chance to fill that position, and my request was granted. I didn't stay *let go* very long at all. I'm now making raspberries at Murphy.

The money was better driving than officing. (I know officing is not a real word, but I made it up and I'm using it.) The dedicated run required me to pick up a loaded trailer in Elgin, Illinois and deliver it to the international terminal in Laredo, Texas. There I would wait until another loaded trailer to clear customs and be shuttled across the border from Mexico. After inspecting the trailer and signing the paperwork, I would transport this trailer to a warehouse in Cincinnati, Ohio. Picking up an empty trailer, I'd head for home, and a couple days off. The whole process would take about five days. I got plenty of rest, drove plenty of miles and was climbing out of the debt pit I had been tossed in by the fiscal irresponsibility of wife three. I also had most weekends free which allowed me to see more of Nancy. We may have been in our 50s, but we still could make yummy sounds.

I requested a week off. Nancy also requested a week off from her job. We packed my Pontiac and headed for South Dakota. I impressed Nancy with my ability to travel to such exotic destinations as The Corn Palace in Mitchell, and Wall Drug, also in South Dakota, without once consulting a map. We strolled through the 1870s ghost town and tourist attractions. We drove through the Badlands which look like a moonscape, no trees, nothing but a gray landscape with breathtaking topography. We drove past prairie dog cities and took pictures of the little critters as they sounded the alarm and retreated underground. We visited the monument at Mount Rushmore and checked on the progress being made on the mountain being carved that will someday become a depiction of the great Sioux leader Crazy Horse.

On our return trip, Nancy patiently followed me as we visited the Old Pioneer Auto Museum in Murdo, South Dakota. We were going to visit the Spam Museum in Austin, Minnesota, but alas, we arrived just after closing time, so the best we could do is take a few snapshots and head for home. We vowed to make it back there when it was open. It's been 10 years and we haven't made it back yet, but we have time. It was a glorious trip that cemented our relationship. Even when I found out that Nancy can't swim and is, for this reason, afraid of water, I was still falling in love with her. Nancy laughed at my jokes, still does. She makes me laugh too, and I need to laugh.

I received an email. It was an inquiry about my present work status. I was being offered a job to head up the transportation section of a small manufacturing business. The salary mentioned would be more than I was making driving to Texas and back. A steady five days a week, eight hours a day job. I had been lured over to the dark side. I gave notice at my old company and started officing again. As mistakes go, this ranks right up there with Custer when he said, "Come on boys, let's ride over and see what the Indians are doing this afternoon."

The company was a family business, run by a father and son. The son emailed me, interviewed me, and hired me. He failed to consult his father who was on an extended vacation in Florida. When the dad returned, all tanned and rested, the excrement hit the blower. He expressed his displeasure with his offspring in rather graphic terms. Then he turned his wrath towards yours truly. He and I were roughly the same age and height. I probably outweighed him by 30 lbs., and I didn't have a spare tire midsection. I could still bench 300 lbs. and it showed. I stood up to him in a way his son never could. I told him point blank that I did not care who he was, nor how much money he had. I didn't care if he wanted to fire me then and there. I had been out of work plenty of times in my life. I further stated that I would not tolerate being verbally assaulted by him or any member of his staff or family. I then said that if he ever wanted to threaten me, I would be incredibly happy to take up the matter with him, man-to-man, wherever or whenever he chose. These words were spoken in a loud and clear, but not yelling, voice out in the loading dock. I was heard by drivers, as well as the manufacturing workers, loaders and the office staff who were peeking out of office doors. The patriarch backed down. He did raise his voice to me on occasion and I raised my voice back at him. But he never swore at me ever again. He didn't like me, and it showed. I was given tasks that were well below the job I was hired to do. I did my best to comply.

I was tasked with hiring two new drivers for the small fleet of trucks being used. I asked about hiring practices and was told that the *Old Man* hired whomever he wanted. There were no driver files, no record of certifications, no background checks, no physicals taken, not even a pre-hire drug test. All of these and more are required by DOT regulations. In other words, if the DOT or IDOT ever walked in for an inspection, the entire operation would be shut down until this matter could be brought up to compliance minimums. I pointed this out to sonny boy, who informed his dad. Daddy again hit the roof. He must have thought he was above the law. His son did some research and discovered that I was correct in my appraisal of the problem. I was given a green light in qualifying their present driver pool and setting up a standard policy for hiring new drivers.

The first thing I had to do was convince the old drivers to fill out a job application and the other paperwork that DOT regulations insisted on. There were none of these on file anywhere. I needed copies of their driver's licenses and the DOT required medical cards. There were five trucks and five drivers. None of these five drivers had a medical card. I had to set up a contract at a local clinic to have both the physicals and drug tests administered. Each driver was to have an employment file maintained by the company. I set these up, making a new file and duplicate for each driver. I had to let two drivers go the next day. One was denied a medical card due to diabetes and a severe heart condition. The second one failed the drug test, having tested positive for both Cocaine and Cannabis. A third driver was unhappy about having to comply with what he called the *Fascist Nazi's* that made him jump through hoops to keep the job he had for the past 10 years, so he quit.

I had three seats to fill and fast. I enlisted the services of a temporary job service that specializes in truck drivers. I was sent pre-qualified and pre-drug tested drivers who were ready to work. If a driver worked out well after a month, he or she could be offered a full-time position. Some drivers worked extra hard to try to snatch up one of these plum jobs. Others were happy to take temp jobs, not being tied down to any company.

Freight moved out smoothly. The father expressed his displeasure with the loss of his best three drivers. He also took offense to an actual woman driver that the temp agency sent out. He expressed these objections to his son, but loudly so all could hear. When he turned his anger towards me, it was the last straw. I blew my top. I was outraged and wasn't going to take this kind of treatment from anyone. The verbal offenses were traded and the distance between us grew smaller. When he accused me of performing unspeakable carnal acts with my mother, I stopped. I was maybe a foot away and staring with rage into his eyes. I said in the iciest voice I could muster, "If you would like to continue this conversation in private with no witnesses, I'm ready, but be assured that unless you pull a gun on me, you will not triumph." He flushed even redder than before and ran back to the office where he and his son plotted my demise. Later that day, I cleaned out my desk and after collecting my paycheck, exited the building never to return.

I returned to my apartment just as my phone rang. It was the police from the town where the company was located. I was asked some questions about my former employment status. I was then asked about a recent altercation at the company in question. I told the officer what had taken place and about my subsequent departure. I was then informed that a restraining order of protection was issued and that I was not to come within 100 feet of the company property nor any member of the family who owned the company. I chuckled and told the officer that I would indeed comply. I bid him a "Have a nice day," and hung up. The rage had left me, and now I needed another job.

On Monday morning, I called the temp agency that I had working for me a few weeks before and started working for them. I stipulated that under no circumstances would I ever work for or deliver to a certain company (which will remain nameless). The temp agency official, knowing very well the company and family in question, laughed, and agreed that it would be best for all concerned and we shook hands on it. I was given several good jobs, and I was happy being a temp, dealing with different companies and people who were happy to fill a driver's seat while their employee was on vacation or ill. I was assigned to a large company not too far from my apartment to cover for drivers that scheduled vacations throughout the summer months. I was even offered overtime and Saturday runs.

In late September, I was told that the temp agency would not be working with that company until the next summer. I was offered a position at a toy manufacturing and distributing company located in Joliet, Illinois. The lease was about to expire on my apartment, so it was decision time. I discussed my problem with Nancy and we both decided to sleep on it and see what we could come up with in the morning. Yummy sounds and exhausted sleep followed. When I awoke, Nancy was sitting up in bed watching me. When she saw my eyes open, she announced excitedly, "I have had an epiphany!" I was intrigued, so I did my morning thing that included the ingestion of strong black coffee. We sat down at the kitchen table and she outlined her plan for my future.

Nancy's father was not doing well and could no longer live by himself. He owned the house where Nancy and her brother lived as children. Nancy wanted to move him in with her, so she could cook for him and help monitor his medication. Her brother would come over and assist with the bathing. Now here is where I come in. I would move into his house and fix it up as rent payment. Nice epiphany Nancy. I jumped at the offer. The house was less than three miles from the toy distribution plant. This would be perfect. (IN YOUR FACE, MURPHY!)

When I first entered the house, I was overwhelmed. There was a lot of clutter in every room. Nancy's dad had been struck down with a stroke several years back and his eyesight and hearing were both affected. I had my work cut out for me. The master bedroom had not been touched since Nancy's mother passed 10 years earlier. I moved the old furnishings out, removed the ancient carpet, and painted the walls. With the addition of a ceiling fan and blinds, I could at least have a place to sleep while I worked on the rest of the house. I moved all my stuff into the garage, there was no room for it in the house. I was working nights driving, so I had daylight when I was working on the house. The task was daunting, but manageable. I had help from my soon-to-be brother-in-law, and of course Nancy, who would come by after work to pitch in.

Nancy would take a load of her father's things home with her every day. I would fill the parkway every Wednesday with the things we decided would be discarded. A third portion was set aside and later donated to a local charity like Goodwill. After ripping out the vintage 1970 something carpet, we realized that the carpet padding had morphed into a hard plastic that adhered itself to the wooden floor. Nancy and I spent many long hours on our hands and knees scrapping this stuff off the floor. When that part was done, her brother came in and sanded the wood floors after which we stained and preserved them. They came out very nice indeed.

Nancy and I picked out paint and commenced repainting every room. The color scheme looked great and was suitably matched with the furnishings I had in the garage. A new stove was purchased, as was a new refrigerator. The kitchen cabinets were in great shape, so Nancy brought in some wood soap and set to making them look like new. We worked well as a team; it was fun spending so much time together.

Now it was time to remodel the bathroom. After tearing out the fixtures, it was decided that the best course of action would be to replace the sink and toilet, and salvage the tub. The floor had to be torn up and replaced. The walls were scrubbed down and given three coats of gloss white paint. The plumbing had to be replaced, but having owned houses before, and having the plumbing gene from my grandfather, I set to work. I replaced the old rusting galvanized pipes with copper. There was no shower associated with this tub enclosure, so I installed one. The only hiccup I can remember was when I brought the new vanity that was purchased on sale. (No returns.) It proved too large for the tiny space between toilet and tub. (This particular vanity now resides in the basement bathroom and shower of our present house. My granddaughters have christened it the men's room and are not allowed to enter unless it's a dire emergency.)

Nancy's dad, like a lot of men back in the day, had a shower in the basement. This consisted of a pipe and shower head situated over a drain in the basement. My father had one and my grandfather had one. My dad enclosed his with cinder block and hung a shower curtain. My grandfather just let the water fly wherever it felt like and used a squeegee when he was done. Nancy's dad erected a round shower curtain rod which seemed to work adequately. However, now there was a shower in the upstairs bathroom. No more slippery, sagging, soaking, naked old man shuffling around in the basement. How's that for a verbal picture? Can't get it out of your head, can you? My basement shower has walls, a ceiling, and best of all a door that I can lock from the inside. The word sanctuary pops into my head.

I bought and installed new light fixtures, and ceiling fans. I brought in my flat screen TV. The furniture was in place. Nancy and I cooked her dad's favorite meal. She drove back to her house to pick her dad up. Everything was ready, I was clean, the house was clean, I was holding my breath. The majestic patriarch entered his house and slowly looked around. He kept on progressing to the kitchen where he was ushered to his seat by his smiling daughter. When the meal was done, and it was time for them to travel home, (not far, maybe 10 minutes) Nancy asked her father what he thought of the house? When Leo made the next statement, I was crushed. He said, "It's okay, if you like this sort of thing." Crestfallen. What did I do wrong? I shook his hand and wished him well, with the promise to see him soon. When Nancy saw my distress, she got her dad into the car and came back in to retrieve some *made up* item. She came up to me and said, "That was high praise coming from my dad. He will never tell you that you did a good job. It's just his way." Okay, that made me feel a little better. Later that night, Nancy called me and told me that her dad actually talked to her about how much he really was impressed with our work in his old house. When a few days later, her brother called and let me know that his dad was talking to him about me and all our work, I was happy. Nobody tell Murphy.

I bought a ring and was planning to give it to her for a surprise Christmas present. Her family came over to her house Christmas Eve and started exchanging gifts. I figured this would be a good time to propose and I think it worked. Her dad was there and when I got him alone, I promised to take care of his little girl, and he smiled at me and squeezed my hand. There wasn't a lot of emotion shown in her family, but it's hidden in there, and I understand it now. Nancy is my best friend.

Right after Christmas, my job at the toy distributor dried up. It was not unexpected and I would still have temp jobs, but things were a bit slow. I started looking for another trucking job and found one that appealed to me. I would be hauling cars from the Midwest to the West Coast, with loads coming right back to the Chicagoland area. This could work. I could check in on my parents, see Paul make, some money and head back home. Nancy was very busy taking care of her dad and we were spending less time together, so this was a way to keep money coming in. I decided to give it a shot. How hard could it be?

Hauling cars is hard. I drove an eight car enclosed truck trailer combination. I had to learn how to load and unload cars, strap them down for safety, find my way to my destination, unload the cars at multiple stops, collect the money, and do it all over again for the trip home. All the while, I was keeping a legal logbook and making sure the load of cars was distributed properly on the truck so the weight over each axle didn't exceed the weight limits. What have I gotten myself into this time? Well, I was never afraid of hard work, so I persevered. The truck I was assigned to was not what you would call the queen of the fleet. It had no power to speak of and it tended to rattle my bones. The sleeper was small, and the mattress lumpy. At least the radio had a CD player, and I was allowed to install a power inverter to run my refrigerator, microwave, and the essential coffee pot. I also had a laptop computer and a small printer that facilitated the sending and receiving shipping documents for the cars to be picked up. Ain't technology wonderful?

I transported some very cool cars with that truck, like one-of-a-kind hot rods, and customized cars. New exotic cars like, Lamborghini, Maserati, Bentley, and Maybach. Vintage cars, from the '40s, '50s, and muscle cars from the '60s and '70s. I even had to learn how to drive a 1926 model T. That was the fun part of the job. The not-so-much-fun part of the job was loading and unloading in all types of weather. In winter, I would load eight cars onto my rig in freezing temperatures. Snow would cover my cars and my footing on the truck was precarious at best. I had frozen fingers and toes, muscles aching from the exertion associated with climbing and strapping down cars. Now there was driving. I thawed out. Slept like the dead in the tiny sleeper with the lumpy mattress.

When I woke up, I headed for my first delivery. I was now in Las Vegas, Nevada. It was early evening, and the outside air temperature was 110 degrees. The Classic 1963 Shelby autographed on the glove box by Carrol Shelby himself, was in the nose of the rig, so I had to unload four cars in the 110-degree heat to get to this one beauty. This Cobra was not a reproduction nor a restoration; it was purchased at auction for $1.12 million. I was a bit shaky when

I accepted the signed documents, the shipping fee, and a nice *tip* for my efforts. I procured a nice clean air-conditioned motel room with my tip money. Showered, belly full of Las Vegas buffet food, I crawled between the sheets and slept for a blessed 14 hours. This was very hard work indeed, but it did pay well.

On one of my trips heading back home, I received a phone call from Nancy. Her dad was in the hospital. He had fallen and hit his head on her bathtub. He had to be taken to the emergency room by ambulance. After fixing his head, it was determined he should stay in the hospital for observation. The next day the hospital released him, and he went back home with Nancy. By the time I made it home, Nancy informed me that her dad was back in the hospital, but this time he was also in hospice. The prognosis was grave, and we were told to gather the family. I was there, even though I was not a family member yet. I did what I could to comfort Nancy. When the doctor came in, he told us that he didn't think that father/grandfather would see the morning, and it would be the time to say goodbye. I got on my phone and called Father Ed from my parish, who came right over to administer last rites, and lead the family in prayer. Tears were shed as they said their goodbyes. Leo's eyes moved from face-to-face, acknowledging each teary set of eyes looking back into his. Leo was on his final journey away from his suffering and constant pain. He was going home to God.

The funeral was a simple ceremony at a small Catholic church in Joliet. There was no music planned, so I asked Nancy if it would be alright if I planned and sang for her father's Mass. She wrestled with whether she wanted me next to her in the front pew or wanted me to sing. She would have her children and her brother with his family around her, so it was decided that I would sing. I had been singing in church since the boys' choir back in fourth and fifth grade, but Nancy's family didn't know that. I enlisted the parish pianist and led the songs for the Mass. This is when I found out that Nancy's family did not sing. Seeing nor hearing anyone joining me in song was a little unnerving but I made it through. At the small dinner after the cemetery, Nancy's brother came up to me, handed me a whiskey, and paid me the best compliment I had ever received. He took my hand in a firm handshake and said, "Ed, that was awesome." Coming from a member of Nancy's family, this was very high praise indeed. I have received accolades prior to and since, but my soon to be brother-in-law's *Awesome* ranks, very high praise indeed. I'm so grateful I was accepted into this unique family dynamic, and happy to be there to help when it was needed.

For the three years prior, Gabe and his little family had been stationed in Okinawa. I missed seeing Jordyn grow up for those long three years. Pictures were great and talking to a 4- and then 5-year-old was difficult, so when Gabe told me that they were heading back to the states, I was overjoyed. He would be going to recruiter's school, in San Diego, California. This school is 37 days long, so LeAnne and Jordyn stayed with my sister Toni, while Gabe was at school. After the school was completed, Gabe received his orders, and I was again bowled over by the news that the little family troop was being sent to the recruiting station here in the Chicago area! He asked me if there was someplace they could stay until they found a place of their own. I consulted Nancy and it was agreed that they could stay in the house where I was living. I immediately repainted the small bedroom in little girl colors of pink and green. I hauled my desk from what was going to be my office to the basement and started transforming it into a little bedroom fit for a fairy princess. I kept my bedroom and fixed up the second largest room for Gabe and LeAnne.

I wasn't there much. I was still driving and mostly staying at Nancy's when I was home. I managed to visit them as much as I could and played with Jordyn who loved her room. This was great! We read stories and sang songs, real grandpa stuff. (Jordyn couldn't say Grandpa when she was first talking so, from that time until now (17 years later, I am known by my grandkids as Bapa, and I love it.)

A few years earlier, when I left that miserable father and son company, I tested for the State of Illinois Department of Transportation (IL DOT). I did not hear back from them until a year before when I was offered a part-time, winter job as a snowbird. I let them know that I was only interested in full-time employment, thanked the young lady, and figured that was that. A year later, I was getting weary hauling cars, so I filled out an application to drive for a local freight company. I passed the tests and jumped through their company hoops. I would be given a start date when I gave notice at the car transport company. Hands were shaken and phone numbers were exchanged. I would let them know within the next 10 days. This would be my last run hauling cars. It was a very memorable one too.

I had four cars already loaded for California. I was sent into the city of Chicago and informed where to pick up the other four. There was a Mercedes S500, there was a Bentley, there was a Lamborghini, and a 1968 Mustang Shelby Cobra, all picking up and dropping off at the same locations. That sounded easy. I picked up these beauties at Wrigley Field. The cars were going to Arizona just outside Phoenix. These were Cubs' cars! The Mercedes and the Lamborghini, belonged to Carlos Zambrano, ace pitcher and a pretty good batter. The vintage Mustang belonged to Sean Marshal, another up and coming pitcher. The Bentley was owned by first baseman, leading hitter, and gold glove winner Derik Lee. Amazing! I was hauling cars for my beloved Cubs. What a way to end my car hauling career.

When I returned to home base, I called the local freight company and left a message for the person who hired me and was going to give me a start date. While waiting for his return call, my phone rang. I didn't recognize the number, but I answered it anyway. It was a number in Schaumburg, and it was the Illinois

Department of Transportation. They were offering me a full-time position as a Highway Maintainer. Full-time! Home on weekends and paid holidays. Sick days. Health benefits and more! I jumped at this opportunity. (I sure hope Murphy isn't reading this.) Then I got the next call; it was from the person who was about to hire me at the local freight company. I apologized and thanked him for the chance to work for his company. I told him that I would indeed call him if this new job didn't pan out. It panned out.

I finished my last trip with the car hauling company, collected my last paycheck and turned in the company equipment. I cleaned out my truck, which was more than the last guy did for me. I had a lot of stuff in that truck. My car was full, and Nancy's car handled the excess. I would be home every night. I had a week to relax and goof off until my new job started, and I took advantage of every minute of the time I was allotted. Gabe and his little family had purchased a house close by, and I helped them get settled. Mostly I played with Jordyn and kept her out of the way. It's good to be the Bapa.

Chapter Fifteen: A Brother Marine

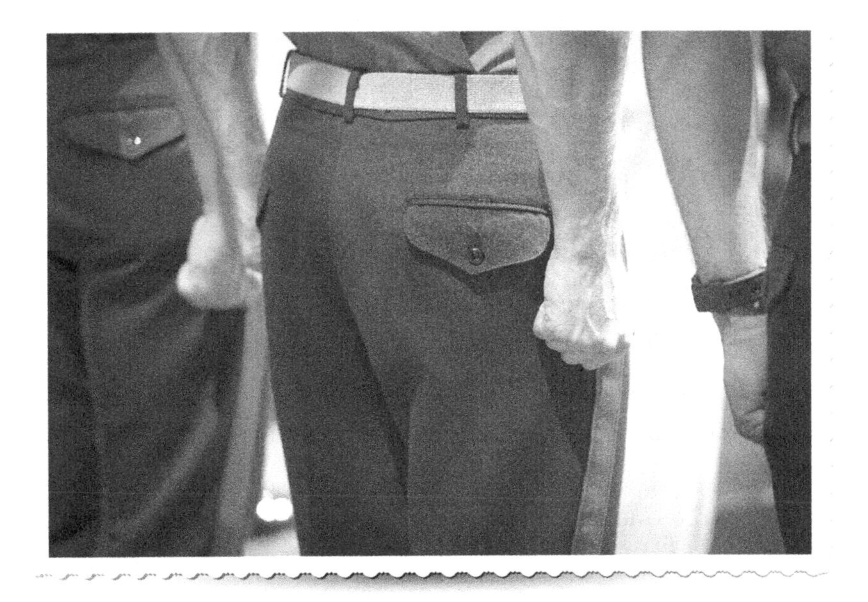

The little house in Joliet was mine again, but it was a little lonelier. Nancy's daughter and new son-in-law were moving up from New Orleans and needed a place to live. I was persuaded to move in with Nancy. (Didn't take much of an arm twist on her part.) A rent amount was established, and the couple moved in. I rented a storage locker and filled it with the stuff that would not fit in Nancy's house. I was ready to start a new chapter of my life working for IDOT.

I sat through a 2-day orientation up in Schaumburg and on March 16th, I showed up at the Naperville Maintenance yard, ready for duty at 6:00 a.m. in the morning. The drive was easy with no traffic to speak of. Being released at 3:00 p.m., the return commute was also quiet. This wasn't too bad at all. In March, the state still considered it snow-and-ice season, so there were still many seasonal snowbirds working at the yard. I didn't know one worker from another nor did I know what to do when assigned to my first pothole crew. This was so alien to my former working life. We signed in at 6:30 a.m. At around 7:00 a.m. we were assigned to a crew. At 7:45 a.m. or so, we left the yard and headed to our designated work area. At 9:00 a.m. it was break time, so we took our union mandated 15-minute break. We worked until 10:45 a.m. when we headed to an agreed upon lunch spot, where between 11:00 a.m. and 11:30 a.m. we ate our lunches. At noon, we headed back to our work area where we worked until the afternoon break at 1:15 p.m. This break usually lasted until around 1:45 p.m. We were back in the yard at 2:00 p.m. where we put the trucks and the rest of the equipment in their designated places, washed up and waited for 3:00 p.m. to roll around. So, in fact we worked a total of two-and-three-quarter hours, out of the eight hours we were paid for. I had been used to driving 12-hour days and putting in 10 days until I got a break. This was more like retirement, than work.

The first six months at IDOT was a probationary period. We newbies were assigned lesser tasks such as, cleaning trucks, picking up litter, and filling potholes. We were seldom allowed to drive the trucks. We were not allowed to operate any of the power equipment. As the weather turned warmer, and the snowbirds left for their summer jobs, we newbies were gradually assimilated into the ranks of the full-timers. (The distinction between full-timer and snowbird is almost like the difference between NCOs and privates in the military.) We, as full-timers are supposed to dislike snowbirds and to treat them as second-class citizens. I think that is a rather dumb practice, but a practice still prevalent today. These men and women come to work. They come to work for IDOT, instead of collecting unemployment when they are laid off from their regular jobs. They are paid less than full-timers for doing the same thing all winter that we did. When the snow starts flying, these dedicated, able-bodied, hard-working snowbirds are out one the streets and highways clearing the snow and ice. They are often assigned trucks that are older and are less comfortable. Full-timers are assigned the new trucks. We all work side-by-side during the worst snowstorms that Mother Nature can throw at Northern Illinois. Yet at the end of the season, when these full-time temporary employees, (The official term for snowbird in the IDOT vernacular is full-time temporary.) leave for the summer months, they are not revered, they are bad-mouthed. I don't understand this practice and like bigotry, I don't think I ever will.

The Naperville yard had its cliques, outcasts, and bullies. The guys who were there for a few years resented us newbies. Our batch of new workers were all veterans and were seen as having been given special treatment in hiring. The other thing was we were not used to the lax way that the others went about their daily tasks. We were all considered over achievers, and I guess we were. I was used to working long days without breaks. I found that filling my day with actual work made the time go by faster. This was not the IDOT way. Oh, silly me.

There were some characters in the Naperville yard, practical jokers, old hippie types, red necks, and several Vietnam Vets. There were a few lead workers who were not exactly leaders, and certainly not workers. One of these was who you would call a *point and blow horn*, lead worker. Most days there was a pothole repair crew out hunting for these tire flattening, rim bending, hub cap tossing little devils. Mr. Horn-Blower would follow the men with the shovels and hot asphalt wagon, and point out potholes from his air-conditioned pickup truck, while leaning on the horn. On cooler days, he would have his windows open, so he could shout at the slow, lazy, incompetent, poor excuse for a highway maintainer. Of course, the language used was often vulgar and sometimes alluded to the sexual exploits of our forebears, and yes, body parts. This was not the way to motivate people to work better or faster. This was demoralizing and demeaning. Well, at least we got weekends off.

One day, one of our practical jokers decided it was time to see if he could stir-the-pot on our little pothole crew. When Mr. Horn-Blower told one of the men on the crew to check the oil and fluids in his pickup truck, Mr. Joker slipped over to the pickup and stealthily removed the fuse that was attached to the vehicle's horn. Whispers and giggles cascaded throughout the yard. When our pothole crew started our hunt, there was, at first, blessed silence from behind us. Then the driver's side window lowered, and the distinctive voice of Mr. Horn-Blower tried in vain to ruin our good mood with his rantings. The loaded and more explicit these verbal offerings became, the wider the smiles of the crew became. Now this was the way to motivate a crew. We filled a lot of potholes that day, and while smiling.

One of the favorite antics of Mr. Joker also involved a horn. The state trucks used for snow plowing in winter are used for many other tasks in summer. These are three-ton and six-ton trucks equipped with air brakes. Air brakes also means there is also an air horn. This horn is extremely loud. It is activated with a cord that hangs above and to the left of the driver's seat. (The arm motion that kids use when encountering a big rig on the road, with little fists in the air pumping frantically up and down, is a request for the Bubba behind the wheel to yank down on the cord, thus blaring this air horn and scaring the bejesus out of whomever is driving the car that carried said kids.) Mr. Joker would climb into the truck from the passenger's side. After crawling over to the driver's side, he would proceed to attach a clear piece of fishing line, from the air horn activation cord to a fixed object inside the cab. He would then carefully exit the truck the same way he entered. The next morning when the truck assignments were given out, Mr. Joker would whisper to a few of his cronies, and they would wander over to the booby-trapped truck and unsuspecting driver. A blaring air-horn, peeling laughter, and many vocal assaults came wafting from the truck bay. I always thought that someone should have been standing by with the defibrillator paddles at the ready for the older and weaker driver victim. I haven't heard of any fatalities from this prank, so I guess it must still be in practice.

There was a gentleman I met at the Naperville yard that proves it is indeed a small world. This guy is a fellow Marine of approximately the same age as me. We got to talking about our Marine Corps careers and found out that we served at the same time. He was in boot camp at Parris Island South Carolina the same time I was, only in a different platoon. From there, he went to infantry training, and I went to my aircraft school in Tennessee. We then were both transferred to Okinawa at nearly the same time. From there, we were both transported to the Philippines where we were assigned to embark on the same ship. The ship was the USS Okinawa and we were heading for the Gulf of Siam in the South China Sea. He was attached to the infantry battalion and I with the helicopter squadron. We never met on board ship that either of us could recall. We shared the same recreational areas, we shared the same mess hall, but if we ever ran into one another, our feeble memories paired with the number of years that have passed, wiped that slate clean. The fact that we both were almost 40 years older and larger didn't help either.

Further conversations revealed more coincidences. We were both involved with the retrieval of the remains of our fellow service members from the jungles of Vietnam in the days prior to the fall of Saigon, in the spring of 1975. He was one of the infantrymen who first accompanied our big green helicopter into the jungle and then out to the waiting hospital/morgue ship where our fallen brothers would await their final trip home; later to have their names immortalized on the polished onyx colored granite slab that was ever to be called *The Wall* of the national Vietnam memorial in Washington, DC. I was trained as a door/tail gunner, and he was one of the solemn-faced young men who would run out the rear of the bird and set up a perimeter for our safety. We would hear more than see any enemies. Now and then, the crack of small arms could be heard above the thrumming of the idling chopper. When we were in the air, none of these rifle reports could be heard, but there were a few times when after returning to our ship, post flight inspection revealed small puncture wounds in the underbelly of our bird. The stench of decomposing and often burnt flesh filled the cabin of our aircraft. Even with the doors and windows open, the dreadful assault on our olfactory organ along with the knowledge of where it came from, was devastating and haunts me to this day. (Hence part of the PTSD mentioned earlier.)

The same brother Marine and I spoke of the evacuations of first Phnom Penh in Cambodia, then Saigon, in Vietnam. (Now called Ho Chi Minh City.) We spoke of the long stress filled day that dragged into night. We shared stories of landing on the embassy grounds and marveling at the sight of so many desperate people of all ages pleading with the perimeter guards to let them onto the helicopters that could transport them away from the certain death that awaited them if they were forced to stay. Cries of, "Please just take my child," could be heard, followed by wailing that could only come from the mouth of a desperate mother. More calls of, "I have money, and I will give it all to you if you take me." There was a cacophony of various languages, voices of a thousand souls beseeching for refuge that we could not give them. This I think, was right up there with the fear of getting shot, or having a mighty helicopter shot down and crashing to earth with all hands aboard, as a source of my own horrible memories of that day.

I witnessed helicopters being pushed off carriers into the sea. I witnessed a brave refugee, when being told he could not land his chopper on the deck of our carrier, hovering just above the flight deck. His young family then leaped for their lives for the safety of the ship. This included two small children, a toddler, and an infant in its mother's arms. The brave father then flew off to a safe distance and jumped into the uncertain waters below, narrowly missing being cut in two by the final death throes of the crashing aircraft. This man was immediately rescued by the Navy and reunited with his family. This loving father was ready to sacrifice himself for his wife and children. A loving man who I pray is enjoying his life here in the states.

On the other side of the coin were the two men who flew an old Army Chinook, (a double-bladed cargo/troop carrier) and landed early on in the operation. They disembarked the craft with the Navy personnel standing by to receive the refugees that were thought to be following. There were none. The cargo bay of this beast was filled with new Hondas motorcycles and accessories from their store. This was one of the first helios that was unceremoniously dumped overboard. Greed motivated these two, so I'm sure they thrived in our land of plenty.

The polarized debate concerning the Vietnam conflict and the United States' role in this conflict is still hotly hashed out today. Whether it was a just or unjust action, whether we as a nation had the right to enter what was fundamentally a civil war, is beside the point. We were there. Our armed forces engaged in this hostility to the best of our ability. The slogan that can be seen on many a bumper sticker, tee shirt, and patches worn on caps and vests reads: *All gave some, some gave all.* Rings so true even now so many years later. It refers to the sacrifice made by all of us who answered the call to arms in support of a less than grateful nation. We were shunned when we returned home. We tried our best to assimilate back into a society that did not recognize us for the true American patriots that we are. It wasn't until our troops were engaged in the recent wars in Iraq and Afghanistan that the nation stood up and the new wave of patriotism flourished across the land. Signs reading, *Support our Troops,* were starting to be seen. American flags were again being displayed all over our neighborhoods. Now people started to include the old gray bearded Vietnam vets with, "Thank you for your service, sir." A little late, but quite welcome.

I had never had a chance to have this conversation, because I had no one who could understand, or so I thought. Dredging up the old memories was the trigger that would, a few years later, lead me to the VA and the help I didn't even know I needed. My father nor my uncles ever talked about their time during World War II. It took me over 40 years to talk about my time in 'Nam. We all tend to downplay our part in all the armed conflicts throughout the ages. We justify this by saying, "I wasn't actually in combat, the guys in the meat grinder every day did all the really nasty stuff. The bullets missed me, and I came home in one piece." Well, it's not so. A lot of us experienced things and saw things that most people, thank God, never did, and should pray they never will. It haunts our dreams and sometimes our wakefulness. It damages our relationships. It makes being around people difficult. Jobs are hard to hold on to. We are called mean, brooding, and can't work well with others. Our depression grows, until we either lash out in fury, or run away and embrace solitude. Still others take solace in the bottle or drugs, always looking for answers, but not even knowing what questions to ask. I didn't want to get dark or melancholic, but there I go, doing it anyway. Sorry.

In my first six months at IDOT, I took one sick day. I wasn't sick, but my car was. In all my days of working, I had never called in sick. This is something I learned by example. I can't think of any time that my father ever called in sick. It just never occurred to me. It was an alien concept. I've gone into work sick and was sent home. I planned days off after requesting permission, but never just called in sick. (That is probably why, when I retired from IDOT, I had over 80 sick days on the books that I was paid for.) It turned out to be the best sick day I ever had.

While I was out hunting parts for my ailing Pontiac, I drove past the Joliet yard of IDOT. I had driven by their yard dozens of times in the past, but this time I took notice of it. (The Joliet yard is in Crest Hill, Illinois and has a Lockport address and zip code. I asked the same question you are asking yourselves. Why? No one was ever to give me any kind of an answer. I got a lot of "Just the way it is!" and "That's the state for you." I was never offered a speculation.) I stopped in to introduce myself. I met two of the men in the yard that day. I was then told that there was an individual currently in the Joliet yard that desperately wanted to be transferred to Naperville. I was given his information, and gave mine to be proffered to this individual.

My poor car needed an all-day repair. When I finished, I was beat, sweaty, greasy, and hungry. Nancy made my favorite comfort food: meat loaf, mash potatoes, and corn. After a nice hot shower, I was ready for sleep. Then my phone rang. The man from Naperville was on the other line. We introduced ourselves and he, being a veteran IDOT worker, told me what the process and paperwork would be like for us to change yards. This would be a good thing. I could fill out paperwork with the best of them. I could also follow processes to the letter. I then obtained the required paperwork from the office in Schaumburg. (Everything IDOT comes out of Schaumburg, unless it's truly important, then it comes from Springfield, through Schaumburg.) Paperwork filled out, 'i's dotted t's crossed', it was sent up the chain of command. I was told it should take no more than two or three months. Being a newbie, I settled back and waited.

I mentioned scuttlebutt back in earlier pages concerning Marine Corps gossip. Well, IDOT has their own version, most of which is of course false. I would hear, "Those transfers only happen in the springtime after the snow and ice season." I'd be told, "Requesting a transfer doesn't work, you have to be recommended by the higher ups for that." Finally, I was told, "You have to be working for IDOT for at least five years before they will let you transfer to a different yard." These tales recited by the *lawyers* employed as highway maintainers were disheartening to put it mildly. I decided to ask someone who would have the answers. I phoned the lady in Schaumburg who handled the payroll, our sick days, and our vacation days. (I found it exceedingly profitable to keep in this lady's good graces.) She confirmed the fact that it was difficult to obtain a transfer to another yard simply by requesting one. When I asked her about swapping yards with someone who also wanted a transfer, she exclaimed, "Oh, that's a different story. I can facilitate a swap as soon as the proper paperwork hits my desk." It seems that the *yard lawyers*, as well as the guy who wanted to trade yards with me, were all mistaken.

The following afternoon, I received the right paperwork from my new best friend. I filled out my portion and contacted the man I was going to swap with. A few days later, I was called into the boss's office in Naperville where I was instructed to report to the Joliet yard the following week. Oh, Happy Days!!! Joliet yard is only four-and-a-half miles from home. I would not have to pay four $1 tolls for my commute every day. This was like getting a nice raise in pay. I decided I should treat myself and buy a new car. My trusty old Pontiac had seen better days, and with the money I would be saving on gas and tolls, I could swing a modest car payment.

I took Nancy car shopping. We headed to a local Ford dealership, where I started looking at new Mustang convertibles.

I always had a thing for convertibles, and I hadn't owned one since my 1978 Fiat Spider. I also remember when the first Mustang came out and one was offered as the top raffle prize at our church carnival in the summer of 1964. Dad had walked around the small sports car and with exasperation exclaimed, "$3,000 for that little piece of excrement? It will never catch on. If I were to win that thing, I'd sell it back and buy a new station wagon." The new ones these days are a little higher in price. I looked and drooled over these new chariots. Then I noticed Nancy was not sharing my enthusiasm for these magnificent specimens of Detroit steel. "Don't you like Mustangs?" I asked. To which she replayed, "If you bought one of those, you'd look like an old man trying to be a teenager." She had a point, so we kept looking.

In the used car section of the same Ford dealership, I spotted a medium gray convertible sitting at the front corner of the lot. I slowly made my way over to it and saw that it was a BMW 330ci. Sweet ride! I started walking away when the salesman came up and offered me the keys, saying, "Take her for a spin and let me know what you think." I opened the car and let Nancy in the passenger side. The leather seats felt like a lounge chair. The engine turned over with a deep, but smooth rumble. When the salesman came back, after taking a copy of my license, we were ready for our test drive. The response and power of this little car made my old Pontiac feel like Dad's old station wagon. The BMW cornered like it was on rails. When we got back to the lot, a smiling salesman opened the door for Nancy and taking the keys from me said, "How'd you like it? Sweet ride, huh?" I couldn't argue with that now could I. I timidly inquired about the price and was pleasantly surprised at his response. I could purchase this baby for $2,000 less than the Mustang I had been ogling earlier. I asked Nancy what she thought and her reply was, "In that car, you are stating that you are all grown up, but still know how to have fun." Now you can understand why I married her. I bought the BMW.

Chapter Sixteen: Chicago Winters

When I reported to the Joliet Yard, I drove the Pontiac with a for sale sign on it. I didn't want to show off my new car just yet. I was very well received at my new yard. Better than I had expected, having unwittingly listened to the guy who I swapped with. Turns out he was not very well liked in the Joliet yard, and even if I were an ogre that smelled of swamp scum and had leprosy, I would have been an improvement in their eyes. The Joliet yard was a vast improvement over Naperville. The first thing I noticed was the cleanliness of the place, and there were no rusted hulks of discarded equipment scattered around. The lunchroom was clean and well lit. The restroom was even clean. The offices, though old, were tidy and well kept. Then I was ushered into the boss's office. There was a gaping contrast that ended at his office door. This was like entering a cave, or a hoarder's cabin. It was dark with papers piled on every surface. His desk had stacks of files, making it hard to see the man behind it. I was greeted and given the speech about trying to fit in and not making waves. He handed me a key to the front gate and after I signed for it was told not to lose it. That was it. No other words passed between us. I rarely saw the man because he rarely left his office.

I found the rest of the yard, including the trucks, were also kept cleaner than any I was at the Naperville yard. This would be a nice change from the hoard of misfits I just left. These guys seemed to work together and seemed to enjoy being here. I was taught the boundaries of this new team section and toured all the snow routes that were maintained by the Joliet yard. I quickly learned which roads were ours and the boundaries of each route. The following week the snowbirds were brought in, and my first snow and ice season started.

This group of birds, most of which had been doing the snowbird thing for several years, were for the most part a hard working, jovial and helpful group. Yes, there were a few jokers and a few who found ingenious ways to get out of work. There were many private cubbies where one could hide and nap, until they were missed and they would be found, reprimanded, and sent back to work. I discovered the old fishing line on the air horn bit was not exclusive to Naperville. I discovered, (the hard way) that the wad of grease under the door handle trick was great fun, as long as you weren't the one who found such goo under your door handle. Pin holes were punctured on the underside of Styrofoam coffee cups.

Gloves were turned inside out and stuffed one inside the other. The one that endures today, comes at the end of the day when we are all waiting outside for the word to go home to be announced. The unsuspecting victim is told that his presence is requested by the boss. If timed right, the victim walks into the office just as everyone is told to go. There never was a summons by the boss, and everyone has a big laugh on the way to the parking lot.

My first snow season was a brutal one. We were called out so many times in December and January that Nancy almost forgot who I was. When I was assigned to the night shift, it was normal to be called out just as we were settling in for the night, I wouldn't be back until morning, at which time I would pass out for as long as I could, sometimes being called back at 5:00 or 6:00 p.m. to work another 12-hour shift. I worked both Christmas and New Year's. The best part about it was the overtime checks. Time-and-a-half for working more than eight hours in a day, double time when working on Sunday or a holiday, and triple time when a holiday falls on a Sunday. I was flabbergasted. This was more money than I had ever made. I would never turn down the opportunity to work as many hours as they let me. There were storms on just about every weekend in January, including a storm on the Martin Luther King, Jr. holiday.

Then came February and the second largest one-day snowfall in Chicago history. Three days of constant plowing shifts, 12 hours on and 12 hours off. Then the cleanup started with the pushing back of the huge piles of snow that blocked intersection sight lines. When the weekend came, the day shift changed to night shift which came with an 18-hour shift on Sunday. There were more storms that had to be worked, and by the end of March, we were all exhausted. Our bank accounts were healthy, but our bodies were fading. The snow piles were slowly melting away as spring crept onto the scene. The birds were dismissed, and it was now time to clean up the yard, remove the snow gear from the trucks, and get ready for spring inspection.

Working only 40 hours a week was a refreshing change from the rigorous toils of the winter. Being engaged in the labor of cleaning trucks inside and out, repairs of lighting and other electrical faults caused by the accumulation of salt on, in, and around the trucks, kept us all busy. Getting off at three every afternoon and no weekend work was nice too. Many weekends were spent camping at one of the many state parks in our area. (Okay, we didn't *actually* camp. We have a 31-foot motorhome. We just like getting away and sort of communing with nature with all the comforts we can drag with us.) With my vacation day accumulated, we were able to go on some very nice get-a-ways.

Chapter Seventeen: Travel Adventures

Paul was at school in California. Toni encouraged him and helped him with setting up his curriculum. At this time, Toni was the Vice President of the college Paul attended, so she could also point him in the right direction to secure grant money and scholarships that he took full advantage of. Paul studied hard and earned very good grades. When he graduated in the top 10% of his class, I was so proud of him I could bust. Nancy and I flew out for his graduation and witnessed him receiving his diploma from his Aunt Toni, who had tears in her eyes. He then received the *Man of Distinction* award to thunderous applause. (Mostly from all the family members who came to honor this extraordinary young man.)

Then Paul dropped a bombshell. He had applied and been accepted to finish his baccalaureate degree at John Cabot University in Rome, Italy. What an opportunity! Once again, Toni helped him procure grant money and fill out the proper paperwork. Paul and his girlfriend, who was an art major and attending the same school, were going to spend the next few years in Italy. They had both studied the Italian language in their past couple years at Fullerton College, so they were prepared. They had plans to fly to Oklahoma to visit her family, then drive up to Chicago. The entourage stayed with us for a couple days, then the Oklahomans left for home. Paul and his lady had plans to stay another week before embarking on their Italian excursion. Paul had a lot of friends in Chicagoland from when he lived in the city, so they had many plans. At this time, Gabe, LeAnne, and Jordyn were still on recruiting duty in the area. Now I had an epiphany of my very own. Nancy and I, who were planning to get married in the near future, could accelerate our nuptials, and tie the knot while both my boys were in the same place. Who knew when my two globe-trotting offspring would be in the same, state, or country for that matter? Nancy was agreeable and we set to work planning one of the fastest yet nicest little weddings ever.

The plans started on a Monday morning August 23rd. The license was issued. We then made plans with a local Italian restaurant who promised they could accommodate our little party. One of my work friends' sisters was a pastry chef who offered her talents for the friends and family discount. Nancy was working, cleaning one of our local museums, and she told her friend and occasional lawyer, of our plans to wed this coming Thursday. He expressed his happiness for us, and then said, "Nancy, you know I am a Judge now and would be most happy to perform the ceremony if you'd like." Nancy agreed with a big smile. Next, he offered to conduct the ceremony in the garden right outside his office. This would be a beautiful setting and we both readily agreed. Everything was set up in three days!

The night before the wedding, my two sons and I celebrated by sharing a sumptuous meal at a Brazilian steak house, followed by drinks at the American Legion. We shared stories of days gone by and made plans for when we could all three gather again for more stories. Paul took it upon himself to act as our designated driver, so Gabe and I took advantage of the drinks sent our way by various patrons hearing about this impromptu bachelor party, a night that I will cherish for as long as my memory holds true.

We had a beautiful wedding with most of our family members in attendance. (With the exception of the California clan, they had been to enough of my weddings.) My two sons acting as co-best men, and Nancy's son and one daughter, plus one grandchild Cecelia, 'CC,' who was only four months, were in attendance. Her eldest daughter could not be there but had a good excuse. She was in the hospital about to give birth to her daughter Kenzie. We had natural flowers in this pretty little garden setting. The aroma filled us with the joy of the day. Nancy's brother gave her away, and with smiles and tears they embraced. (Nancy had the tears, not her brother.) The dinner afterwards was also very classy for such short notice. We ate and drank. Toasts were given, more tears were shed. We pulled it all off in three days. We both went back to work the next day. Neither of us saw the need to take two days off in a row just to stay at home. We could take a honeymoon trip another time. We have a plaque in our kitchen that reads, 'It's never too late to live happily ever after.' We are proving that its true.

When the subject came up about an upcoming Hawaiian trip that my family was taking, we jumped at the chance. We were celebrating Mom and Dad's 60th Wedding Anniversary. The family vacation was planned. Five couples were to embark on this Hawaiian adventure. Mom and Dad, Toni and John, Karen and Rich, their daughter Lori and her boyfriend Darin, and Nancy and me. Toni had a timeshare, so the accommodations were very frugal. Karen and Rich volunteered to sit through a timeshare sales pitch to help defray the cost even further. (They had no intention of purchasing, but don't tell the timeshare people.) We were to share a pair of luxury condos fully furnished, including kitchens, on the big island of Hawaii near the town of Kona. We would have 10 days to explore and relax, play in the waves, and sample the local cuisine. Sounds great, doesn't it? Well, yes, in most ways it was fantastic. In a few ways, not so much.

Nancy and I would fly to California, and after a short visit with family who would not be joining us, we would take off to the tropical paradise we had been dreaming about. This first leg of our journey was pleasant and uneventful. We visited and got ready for our next, longer flight. For a reason known only to the airline personnel who made these decisions, we were crammed into an airplane that wasn't meant to accommodate many mostly large passengers in comfort for a five-and-a-half-hour flight. Next came the debacle when this airline wasn't prepared for the two members of our party who had to be transported via wheelchair. (Both Toni and Mom had difficulty walking.) We also had one member of the clan detained by airport security. This had to do with brother-in-law Rich's knee replacement setting off the metal detector. Smushed together like the proverbial sardines, we took off. I was in pain all the way there. My right shoulder ached with a yet to be diagnosed rotator cuff tear. The alcohol offered helped a little, but there wasn't any way to hold my arm that didn't hurt. This was one of the longest five-and-a-half-hour flights I've been on to date.

When we arrived in Hawaii, we realized that the full-sized van that Toni reserved would not accommodate all of us, our luggage, and the wheelchairs. Luckily, the rental company was able to rent us another vehicle. Now we convoyed over to the Hilton resort which was just down the road. The black lava covered landscape wasn't exactly what I had pictured in my mind. As soon as we turned into the resort, things changed. There was an abundance of greenery with flowers and palm trees all over. Okay, this was more like the paradise I had in mind. After settling into our rooms, an excursion to Costco was embarked upon. It was agreed that, when practical, we would relax, and the men would prepare meals. The resort furnished us with a BBQ grill and kitchen full of all the culinary accoutrements needed. I was to oversee breakfast, which was fine with me. I love breakfast and no one can prepare my breakfast in the way I like it better than me. Besides, if I did breakfast, I wouldn't have to do anything the rest of the day except eat and relax. Of course, we ate out a lot, but it was nice to make our own meals too. The local fair was abundant, high in fat, and a tad on the expensive side.

Now it was time for our first trek to check out the touristy spots in Kona. Toni and John had been here a few times before, so we followed their lead. Toni couldn't drive and John was not inclined to, so Rich and I drove in tandem wherever we went. John in the passenger seat in the van with Rich driving, and me driving the second car usually with Nancy, Lori, and Darin. John would navigate for the little convoy of gawking tourists. At this point we came to the realization that John was directionally challenged. He would say to Rich, "We'll have to turn right up ahead." Rich would move the van to the right lane and prepare to turn. I would follow suit right behind him. John would then exclaim, "I said turn right here. Turn left, right here." We would then careen across the road to turn left and bewildered, I followed. This happened more than once, and after we got used to John's rather peculiar method of directions, we started having fun with it. At the end of some of our drives to the best tourist spots on the island, we would all have great laughing fits at John's expense. He took this in stride. He knew we all loved him because we never teased people we didn't like.

Nancy doesn't swim, so she stayed back with Mom and Dad, while Karen, Rich, Lori, Darin and I went snorkeling and swimming with wild dolphins. This was one of the highlights of my trip. I hadn't been snorkeling since Okinawa. Our guides were a trio of young tanned well-toned ladies. They seemed to be paying particular attention to me. Not that I minded the attention, mind you. This was just a little too weird. Then Rich started laughing and the jig was up. He had surreptitiously made it known to the head guide that I was rather feeble and would require a lot of help. We had a good laugh together. I had to get him back. Swimming with dolphins was a unique experience that if given the chance I would do again in a heartbeat. These sleek creatures are as curious about us as we are of them. You can feel the sonar vibrations and hear their clicking and whistling when they come close. Fantastic! Snorkeling the coral reef was an explosion of color that danced and flickered in the sunlight above. So many fish of so many different colors were right there before our eyes. Wonderful and exhausting. An afternoon nap was in order.

This is when I realized that even though a liberal amount of sunscreen had been applied and reapplied that morning, I was burnt. Aloe was obtained and my reddened body was anointed by my loving wife. We spent the rest of the evening and night playing cards and self-medicating with whiskey and beer. Okay it was just Rich and I, drinking whiskey and beer. The ladies sipped wine. Dad and John didn't drink at all, and Lori and Darin were out on their own for a while. We were not exciting enough for the young people, I guess. Rich and I were sitting by the pool reliving the day of colorful fish, dolphins, and the young women in bikinis. (We may be old, but we're not dead.) As I looked at my brother-in-law, I noticed he wasn't wearing a shirt. He was, however, covered with an extra layer of hair across his upper body. Without his shirt off, he looks like he is wearing a fuzzy sweater. I then observed that this hair was graying from his neck to the center of his chest and he had dark sunglasses on. I started calling him Panda, we laughed, had another drink, and laughed some more. I still call him Panda.

We took an excursion on a glass bottomed boat trip at dusk one evening. There was a local band on board and the food was marvelous. (I usually don't use words like marvelous in everyday speech, but it seemed appropriate here.) The rum drinks were potent. The sunset was spectacular. There were no colorful or even drab colored fish to be seen as we glided over the calm waters surrounding the big island that night. The captain apologized saying that this very rarely happens here, and then announced that the next round was on the house. Rich, Karen, and I joined in singing with the band and everyone aboard seemed to have a great time despite the lack of any sort of fish.

I found a Harley dealer in Kona that rented motorcycles by the day. Sweet! I reserved one for the following day and planned to ride the island roads with Nancy on the back. We needed a little time away from all the togetherness the past several days. I got up early and Rich dropped me off to pick up my bike. The bike was the same Heritage Softail Classic that I had at home, only quieter and newer. I rode back to the condo to find Nancy still in bed. She had some ailment that, she assured all of us, would pass quickly. All she needed was to rest in bed for a while. She persuaded me not to spend the day sitting around with her, she would be fine if she was just left alone to sleep. So, I toured the island on my own. It was a beautiful day for a ride, and I made the most of it. I guess I was getting too much togetherness too. I needed a shot of solitude which a motorcycle provides. Nancy was feeling better the next morning. I wish we could have enjoyed the ride together.

When our time on the island was over, we packed up and got ready to go. At the airport, we were advised that our flight had been delayed by about an hour. We took this in stride and toured the little shops in the airport. Getting through TSA took forever with Rich's fake knee, Dad's pacemaker, Mom in a wheelchair, Toni in a wheelchair AND metal rods in her back. There was a mix-up concerning baggage weight which we quickly made right. The airline did have the wheelchairs ready and waiting this time. The larger aircraft that we were promised was nowhere to be seen. The delay that we were advised of an hour ago was to facilitate making a small repair on the larger jet, turning out to be a much larger more complicated repair that needed to be certified before it would be deemed airworthy. Not to worry weary travelers, we just so happen to have another conveyance available so your aeronautic adventure will not be further delayed. At this point they wheeled out the same sorry airplane that we were shoehorned into on our way out here. Oh joy.

My right shoulder had not miraculously healed itself, and after carrying bags and baggage, was screaming at me. We were herded onto the shoe box with wings and got to our seats. Rich's leg was in pain and needed to have enough room to stretch it out, so an aisle seat was obtained for him. Mom and Toni were both settled into their seats. The cabin doors closed, but it was soooo hot on the plane that John started having an anxiety attack. There was nothing that could be done here and no amount of flight attendants *there, there,* or request to take it easy would help. Toni sat with him holding his hand and just letting him know she was there with him. The attack subsided and the frazzled flight attendants offered everyone free drinks. This was met by shouts of approval from the tourists that were just sobering up after a long Hawaiian drinking binge, and we were finally airborne. I needed something a little more potent than alcohol.

Toni to the rescue. Karen, knowing of my discomfort,

maneuvered through the partiers to where Toni was still holding John's had and discreetly took two Vicodin tablets from her. She worked her way back to where Nancy and I were crammed and offered me the medication. I took the pills and swallowed them both and washed them down with the last of the whiskey in my glass. It was my third drink, and the first time I ever took Vicodin. Karen told me that I should have only taken one to see how they worked. Well, they worked, and coupled with the alcohol, I didn't need an airplane to fly home. I don't think my arm stopped hurting, but I know I didn't care.

After another lucrative year of snow plowing, our Hawaiian vacation all paid off and money put aside for the next adventure, Nancy and I had decided to go visit Paul in Rome. We would travel with each other and no one else. Ten people on a vacation, even 10 people you love dearly is way too much to bear. We obtained our passports, booked a direct flight from Chicago to Rome. Paul reserved hotel accommodations for us. (Because he knew a guy.) This was exciting. I had not been out of the states since the Marine Corps and that wasn't a pleasure trip. Nancy and I could explore ancient ruins, eat at romantic little cafés, and take in the grandeur that is Roma. This vacation was so much less eventful than the Hawaii trip where the airline was concerned. This was a jumbo jet that had luxurious seating. My shoulder, having healed from the surgery, was not giving me fits of pain. We were served a very nice in-flight meal that included wine. (I spilled the red wine on my light-colored pants halfway into the flight. So, digging into my carry-on bag, I found that I packed a pair of rather new blue jeans. Changing pants in an airliner washroom is best done by contortionist teenagers.)

When we landed at DaVinci airport we were greeted with a sign bearing our names. Paul had arranged for us to be driven to our hotel by another guy he knew. We were conveyed through the narrow streets of Rome in a late model Mercedes. The driver was dressed in a suit. He spoke heavily accented English as he pointed out some of the sights along the way. As we came to rest in front of our hotel, I was skeptical of Paul's accommodations. The driver guy would not accept any money and even helped us in with our baggage. He bid us farewell and wished us a happy vacation. (Those were the exact words he used too.) The outside of the hotel was nothing like the inside. A modern air-conditioned lobby greeted us with sweetly smiling, young Italian women there to help. Okay, Paul's accommodations guy did good. We took the elevator up to our floor and were shown to a nicely appointed room overlooking the Tiber River. Okay, this is the place for the honeymoon we haven't had time for.

Armed with a map of Rome in English, and some directions given to us by our hostess, we ventured out. It was late afternoon and when we walked out the door we were assaulted by an oppressive wave of heat. It was enough to take your breath away after the cool air inside. We hurried back upstairs and donned shorts and lighter shirts. We headed over to where Paul was working, The Abbey Theater Pub. This was an Irish pub in the middle of Rome. Interesting to say the least. We met Michael, the very Irish bartender, and a few of Paul's other friends. We went out to eat with Paul in the Piazza Navona. As we were chatting, I noticed that Paul had developed a slight Irish brogue. In Italy. Paul also shared with us the fact that he had introduced Taco Tuesday to the patrons in and around the Abbey Pub. A California kid, at an Irish Pub in the heart of Rome, Italy started Taco Tuesday. All I needed were a priest and a rabbi to walk in and I think there might be a joke in the making.

We spent a wonderful time wandering around Rome. Paul showed us many of the regular touristy spots and some of the lesser known, yet just as beautiful as the more famous parts. Paul's girl had to leave for the states to try to secure herself a job back home, so we had Paul to point out the many displays of art, with a fair amount of history behind them. Paul also had a guy who worked for a tour bus company, so we were invited to take a bus tour to the wine country in Tuscany at a reduced friends and family rate. Paul knew a bunch of guys.

When our 10 days came to an end, Nancy and I hugged Paul and it seemed like the entire population of Rome and boarded our plane for the long flight home. This 15-hour flight wasn't half as long as that last vacation flight to Hawaii. Also, it was nice to get back to work. I needed the rest after 10 days walking around Rome.

The following snow and ice season, I was offered the opportunity to be a temporary lead worker. I would be responsible for a daily crew of snowbirds and a newer full-timer. We were assigned tree trimming duty. This means we went out armed with chainsaws, pole saws, and a large chipper that would reduce tree branches to mulch to trim back trees from interfering with our roadways. I had a great crew. We got a lot of work done and we also had fun while we worked. We all had nicknames too. I can't explain these because I promised to keep it clean, but the nicknames were *Lotion, Mumbles, Thunderbolt, Lightning, Buster Bolo,* and they called me *El Chapo.* (The guys even got me a John Deere cap and had *El Chapo* stitched on it.) We would tease each other relentlessly, but as earlier stated, my crew could and did more work than any other crew in our yard or any other yard. On Fridays, I would hold a safety meeting. Our safety meetings took place in one of several small restaurants closest to the area we were going to be working that day. We didn't announce these safety meetings to the others in the yard, so as to not draw undue attention to ourselves. We never took advantage of this little bit of well-earned respite. We simply substituted our two 15-minute breaks into one safety meeting. The morale of my crew was always better than any other crew. When we mistakenly had a meeting at the local Denny's and the big orange trucks were spotted by a boss from another yard,

I was asked by our boss not to conduct any more safety meetings ...at Denny's. He was no dummy. He could see the productivity of my crew. He could see how well we worked together, so with a wink and a nod we found less conspicuous places for our weekly safety meetings. The word did finally get out and now the term *safety meeting* means going out for breakfast for a well-deserved meal with friends and co-workers.

Chapter Eighteen: PTSD: There, I Said It

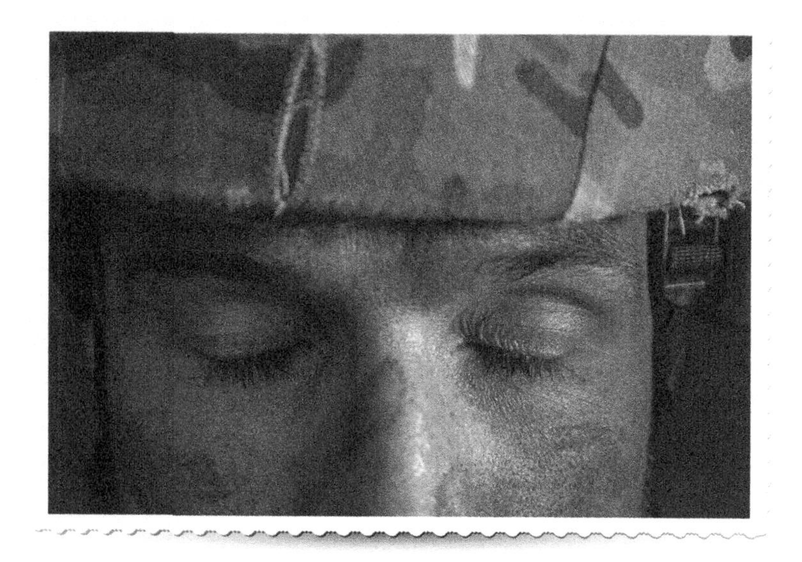

My sister Toni, was fighting a losing battle with cancer. This was a hard time for the entire family. I flew out in early October for a visit before snow and ice season. Toni had insisted on having all of us over for a big family dinner. I showed up at her house, which was filled with all the great aromas of a days' worth of the great cooking she was famous for. When I saw Toni, I knew this would probably be our last meeting. She prepared a traditional Thanksgiving dinner. She was cheerful and cracked jokes as if nothing was wrong. Since I saw her last in the spring of that same year, she had lost over 30lbs, and the cancer was winning the battle. I tried my hardest to stay as cheerful as she appeared, but I was failing in my attempt. I was devastated and I guess it showed. Karen noticed and drew me aside. She was worried about me. I wasn't the one who was wasting away. I wasn't the one who was on the final journey. I told her that and she sighed. The rest of the family had seen this change, but for them it was gradual. It hit me like a runaway truck slamming into a tree.

I traveled home with a pain in my heart that triggered such emotion that it was visible to friends and family. This was my little sister who followed me around when we would play together as not much more than babies. I knew her longer than anyone else in the world, except for Mom and Dad. There were no words that could console me. Nothing in the world could comfort me. Nancy tried, and her kindness softened things only a little. I threw myself into work. I suffered in silence. My crew couldn't cheer me up and took offense at my foul mood. I was then referred to as that grumpy old man. Toni lost her battle three weeks before what would have been her 60th birthday. I was on the phone when the end came. Tears welled up in my eyes as I could hear the crying across the phone line. At least she was no longer in pain. She was with God, waiting for the rest of us.

Dad and Mom experienced the worst thing that a parent ever could; having a child pass on to heaven before them. Dad went to be with Toni next. I was able to write his eulogy and I drove out for his funeral to read it. I made it through without breaking down, and I think he would have been proud. Mom joined them the next year. I couldn't read that one. I was a little too broken. The loss of parents is always a difficult time. It is expected, but you are never ready. The loss of a little sister is overwhelming.

When I returned home this time, I was depressed. Not just a little melancholy, but depressed. I stopped doing the things that gave me pleasure. I stopped going to the gym. I didn't ride my motorcycle. I even stopped going to church. I wasn't angry with God; I just couldn't stand being around people at church. Nancy noticed the change in me and gently coaxed me to seek help. I resisted of course. I would get better, this will pass. It did not. I made an appointment at my local VA. I talked with a doctor, a psychiatrist, who specializes in treating old crusty vets like myself. I was prescribed an antidepressant and made more appointments to visit him. I was also assigned a counselor, who also had a great deal of experience with depressed service members and veterans. At first, I resisted the mention of PTSD. I wasn't in the meat grinder of close combat. How would I get PTSD? Gradually the doctor drew out of me the problems I had been trying to cope with on my own for so many years. The medication was increased and a different prescription was added. I found that talking to these professionals and taking my medication took the edge off. I gradually came to terms with my PTSD and started the long road back. Sorry for delving into darkness again. My life couldn't be all rainbows and unicorns. (Paul will get that little joke.)

We got a new boss at the Joliet yard. He is way different from the boss who never came out of his office, and the last boss who had his own way of doing things that were sometimes less than orthodox. When the new boss questioned me about my lack of motivation, and general lethargy, I gave him the Reader's Digest condensed version of my depression and PTSD. (You kids had better talk with grandpa again and ask about Reader's Digest.) The new boss listened intently and told me he fully understood. He has a brother who suffers from clinical depression and knew a little bit about it. He further told me he would assign me tasks that would allow me to work alone if I needed to. This made my long road back a little less bumpy.

Chapter Nineteen: Happy Campers

After the less than stellar winter season (we didn't get much snow, ergo not much overtime . . .) that year, springtime brought on the next inspection. I was granted permission to set up a system to get all the trucks washed, have all the safety gear checked, and all the lights checked before inspection. Everything would be checked, repaired, and checked again, then checked a third and final time before the inspection day rolled around.

The rest of the crew were at first reluctant to utilize my system. The guys who had been there a while would say, "That's not how we did it before." To which the new boss would reply, "Well, just because you did it one way for years, doesn't mean you have been doing things the right way, or more importantly MY WAY." Our yard received a 100% rating on our inspection. The inspection was in the morning, and we had our traditional cookout in the afternoon. The next day being Friday, the boss conducted a *safety meeting*.

Nancy and I planned a trip for early fall. We would pack up the RV and head south to New Orleans. This was someplace in the U.S. (maybe the only place) I hadn't been to. We could discover the Crescent City together. This was before I purchased the Jeep that we dragged along behind the RV these days. Instead, I attached my small trailer behind the motorhome and loaded my motorcycle inside. This was so we had transportation to and from the state campground we reserved. This worked well in New Orleans, not so much when we stopped in Memphis. This was October, even though it wasn't Chicago in October cold, it was still a little cold for riding a motorcycle. We shivered and our teeth chattered, but we were able to experience some of the touristy stuff Memphis had to offer, ending with a stroll down Beale St. and dinner at BB King's Blues Café. Riding back to the campground was bone chilling and we had a night cap and snuggled into our nice, soft queen-sized bed. Camping indeed.

We both loved New Orleans. Walking down Bourbon Street hearing the smooth jazz and blues wafting out of everywhere was magical. Coffee and Beignets in an outdoor café with a live Dixieland band playing, not having anywhere to be with my love at my side to enjoy it with. Have I used the term priceless lately? We walked all over the French Quarter and the French outdoor market. We ate Muffuletta filled sandwiches for lunch and sampled the finest Cajun cuisine anywhere for dinner. Drinking unfortunately had to be kept to a minimum because of our motorcycle ride back to the camper. Neither of us are very big drinkers, so that wasn't hard to do. We enjoyed this city immensely. We had the opportunity to stroll through a few of the famous above ground graveyards. We visited the new World War II Museum. This is a stunning multimedia attraction that reverently teaches young and old what our brave forbearers went through so we could live and stay free. At one point on the tour, we entered a simulation of an old train as part of our trip to our induction centers. The train was equipped with a movie screen that simulated the trains moving through cities and towns. One of our guides that I had been talking with earlier, said to me, "Look at that car stopped at the train crossing. It's a 1953 Ford. It's the only mistake they made in this whole place." It is a fantastic museum and I recommend everyone to visit when they travel to New Orleans.

After a few days, we left New Orleans and headed toward the panhandle of Florida. This being early October, kids were back in school, and the seasonal wanderers hadn't arrived yet, so we had the entire beach to ourselves. We waded in the light surf and soaked up the sunlight. In no time the weather would be a frigid, snowy mess at home, but I didn't want to think about that now. We had another day to relax and do nothing before heading home. The drive home was uneventful. Instead of a campground we stayed in a truck stop part way home. Nostalgic to me, not so much for Nancy, but she didn't complain. I explained that I had spent many a night in a truck stop being lulled to sleep with the vibrations of the truck. Then I exclaimed, "I love the smell of diesel in the morning." Guess you had to be there.

Nancy and I did more *camping* the following year. We took CC with us sometimes and Mr. Guy, our chocolate lab, with us all the time. Having a dog, especially one like Guy also aided me by getting me up and moving. We would go for walks for sure, but Mr. Guy's favorite thing to do is go to the dog park. He is almost six years old as I write this, but all I have to do is say, "Bye, bye car?" and he is heading for the back door, nails clattering and sliding across the tile in the kitchen. When I open the garage door he jumps and wiggles and gives out happy little yips. He then leaps into the back seat of my Jeep and sits there looking at me as if to say, "Come on already. Start the car. What are you waiting for?" He has a very expressive set of eyes. If it isn't too cold out, I leave the passenger side window open so Guy can stick his head out the window and sniff the air. As soon as I turn the corner, still about a quarter mile from the entrance to the park, he starts bouncing around in the front seat.

A 90 lb. dog bouncing around my Jeep Wrangler makes for a wild sight. When we pull into the dog park, he goes crazy with anticipation. (I'm glad he has a strong bladder at times like this.) I get out on my side and circle around the back of the vehicle, where I find my big dog sitting ever so still. He's giving me his best *I'm a good dog* look when I open the door. He bounds out of the Jeep, takes a few steps, and turns to me and sits until I hand him his favorite toy, a rubber pig that has a distinctive oink squeaker in it. I walk over to the gate, carrying his water dish, a bottle of water, his leash and collar. Guy is now wild with anticipation. Especially if some of his doggy friends are there to play with. I place his bowl and other stuff on a bench and watch him run. This is the time when Guy makes sure I get some exercise too. Guy does what dogs do at the dog park. Guy does his thing as far away as he can while still being inside the confines of the park. I walk all the way out there with a poop bag at the ready and start my do-do hunt. I get distracted when Guy brings his pig for me to chuck for him, so I end up walking around where I think his deposit is until I find it, bag it and deposit it in the container provided. We then proceed to play pig until one of us gets tired. In the winter, I am usually the one who calls it quits when I can no longer feel my fingers. In the heat of summer, Guy, being a dark brown dog, gets hot and lets me know it's time to go home. He expresses his wishes to depart by grabbing his pig and heading for the gate. At times like these no amount of *come here,* or *give me the pig,* has any influence on Guy. His mind is made up. He wants to go home.

After a prolonged rain, the park gets a little soggy, also when snow melts in spring. At times like these, Guy plays in any mud puddle he can find. If he spots a particularly large puddle, he finds joy in wallowing in the same way his favorite toy would, if it weren't made of rubber. Now my chocolate friend is more milk chocolate than his natural dark chocolate self. (This is why he doesn't ride in my BMW.) When he jumps in the Jeep, he shakes great gobs of mud and water all over the interior. (This is why I have washable seat covers in my Jeep.) It's bath time! I drive over to our local farm and farm accessory store, then Guy and I go in. We are here for his bath, though I get wet too. For $9.99, we use the dog wash facility located in a corner of the store. There is a walk-in tub that allows an easy entry. I'd hate to have to lift my muddy mongrel up to get him in the tub. I lift the tub's side panel and Guy jumps in. There is nice, warm water, and several kinds of doggy shampoo. I take along the soft rubber curry brush that helps me work in the soap and work out the mud. Guy is very cooperative, and only fidgets when I have to wash his face.

After a good rinse, I open the tub gate, and 90 lbs. of wet dog jumps out and starts vigorously shaking as dogs have done throughout history. This is when I get wet. I dry him off the best I can with the towel provided and use the industrial size hair dryer to try getting the rest of him dry. He is not overly fond of this part. I spray him down with some doggy deodorant squeegee the shaken dog water down the drain, and we exit the dog wash. We take a few laps around the store while the air dries a little before going back out to the Jeep. Tossing an old blanket over the back seat, I let my clean, not to mention fresh smelling K9 back in. At this point, my Jeep interior smells like dirty dog and almost every surface has mud splatter on it. Now it's Jeep bath time. Then maybe I'll have enough energy to shower my own muddy self.

You ask me, how did you obtain such a wonderful monster of a dog? Well, he comes from a broken home. The young couple who was previously owned by Mr. Guy split up and the young lady got custody. She moved into a small apartment with a girlfriend who was owned by two smaller dogs and a cat. Poor Mr. Guy spent the six months, prior to adopting Nancy, CC, and I, in a cage. He was let outside to do what dogs do outside then right back in. I found out about Guy from the young lady's mother who was the girlfriend of the drummer in the band I had been the sax player for. (I didn't last long in that band because I was only filling in till their keyboard player came back from an injury.) I showed Nancy pictures of Guy, but she was skeptical of such a large breed. She agreed to go meet the young lady and this gentle giant. Her mistake came when she allowed CC, who was six at the time, to accompany us. CC fell in love with this monster. Nancy followed suit. Guy came home with us. I had a new best friend and another male in our house full of estrogen. Guy is great with small children who tend to lay on him, put bunny ears on him, put hair ribbons in his hair, pull his ears and even put their tiny little fists in his mouth. Guy stoically endures this treatment, then when he has had enough, he calmly gets up and hides in the bedroom. (Can you blame him?)

Guy is a great retriever, and would make an excellent hunting dog, if you were a bowhunter. The big dog is afraid of loud noises. Fireworks, thunderstorms, and gunshots send him into fearful trembling. Guy adopted us when he was three, and we are still unable to lessen his fear. When a storm hits, he is dosed with a doggy downer and taken to the basement where the noise isn't as intense. The week before the Fourth of July is especially hard on him. I sit with him in the basement watching movies with the sound up. I do think he likes his drugs though. Maybe he's faking it to get his fix. He's smart, but not that smart.

The summer CC turned six, Nancy and I decided to take her on a trip in the motor home. We were heading out to California to visit my family. Gabe and family were stationed back at Camp Pendleton, and Paul was working in Los Angeles. Gina and Bill were in Long Beach, Karen and Rich in Whittier, and Mom and Dad were in an assisted living house just down the street from them. So, our trip was planned. Vacation days were calculated. The RV was serviced, and supplies were laid in. The excitement built to a fever pitch, and that was just CC, who was promised a trip to Disneyland. Packed and ready to roll, we set off, like our pioneer forbearers, westward ho.

A few years before, when she was four years old, I taught CC, or as I call her *Squeaky*, how to swim. She was and still is fearless in water. This trip would allow her the opportunity to do a lot of swimming. As we traveled, we would pick out campgrounds with swimming pools for Squeaky and dog parks for Guy. I did all the driving because Nancy would not pilot such a large vehicle. She was also way out of her comfort zone, and hated driving on an expressway, freeway, or interstate. After all the years I spent behind the wheel of a big rig, I still love driving, and a 31-foot RV posed no problem at all. The only hiccup came on our second day out, when I called my nephew in Colorado, and we made plans to get together that night. This was not my finest hour. It was a long, long drive for a 6-year-old to have to endure, and Grandma got a little miffed at me for miscalculating the time and distance it would take us to get there. My bad! After the 12-hour day, I vowed to drive no longer than eight hours, before finding a suitable campground for the night. The rest of the journey was much more pleasant. We stopped a lot during the day and set up camp in the late afternoon which afforded us plenty of time to swim and relax. We cooked in the RV a lot of the time, but we ate out now and then too. This driving only during the day was new to me, but nice. I got to see more of the country this way. I had driven this route an abundance of times and missed a lot of the scenery because I drove at night a lot of the time.

We meandered through Colorado, followed the road through Monument Valley in Utah and Arizona. (In all my years of driving I never meandered before.) We witnessed spectacular vistas and camped at the Moab, Utah KOA. It was extremely hot. Dry heat my big toe! It was hot. The pool was refreshing, and of course the RV has air-conditioning, but we didn't cook outside that evening. The sunset was beautiful, and we enjoyed it from the comfort of our little house on the freeway.

When we pulled over in front of Karen and Rich's house, they came out to greet us. CC was amazed that they had a pool right in their backyard. After a little pleading, Uncle Rich took her in back to experience the wonders of his new backyard grotto and pool. This was an artful display, with manmade yet very realistic rock formations forming a waterfall and slide that caused a great deal of squealing to emanate from Squeaky. Lori and CC became best friends at once. Yes, CC was six years old and Lori 30, but they were best friends. They sang *Frozen* songs together and talked about all the Disney movies. It really was sweet. Lori was so good with CC, who she now refers to as her mini me.

The next stop on the cross-country odyssey was Long Beach, where Gina and Bill had a big enough driveway to fit our home away from home. They also had guest rooms, and a swimming pool. You would think Squeaky would be waterlogged by now, but she proves to be our own little mermaid. We found a local dog park and Mr. Guy had the opportunity to stretch his legs, play some pig, and sniff other dogs. Nancy and I even got a night out by ourselves. Gina and Bill volunteered to watch CC and Guy while we went out to dinner. We found a little Italian bistro in a quiet section of Long Beach. We drank wine and ordered Margarita Pizza. We ate al fresco and reminisced about our trip to Rome a few years back. After five days cooped up with a 6-year-old with way too much energy and way too many questions, we needed a break. We love her to death and would do anything for her. Sometimes it gets a little much for a couple of old fogies to handle. That's why God gives babies to young people. Old people get tired.

The next day would be Squeak's big day. Disneyland!!! Gina told us that it was the only thing she could talk about while we were at dinner. Karen's daughter-in-law works security at the *Magic Kingdom*, so we were able to enter the park with the friends and family discount which is one of the perks Disney employees get in their incentive package. So, not only was I now the hero and best Bapa ever, but I also got to take Nancy and CC into the happiest place on earth, for FREE? (Nice discount huh?)

We went into the 'California Adventure' side of the park. This side had rides and attractions depicting the more recent Disney movies, cartoons, and other animated TV shows popular with the 4- to 10-year-old crowd. *Toy Story, Little Mermaid, Cars*, and *A Bugs Life* all had rides that would transport the rider into the movie with songs and colors and talking animatronic characters. There was a dance party attraction that combined a large movie screen showing the most popular TV show with live costumed characters that would pop out of the movie and dance with all the little ones, while the parents and grandparents enjoyed the cool air being pumped in.

The next attraction, and CC's favorite by far, was *Frozen*. This was a live stage play with the background depicting scenes from the movie as only a team of Disney professionals could pull off. Squeaky was in her glory. This was right in her wheelhouse. I have never seen a little girl having so much fun. She sat on my lap to see better. By the end of this production, she was bouncing, clapping, laughing, squealing, with tears in her eyes, and all at the same time. We then waited for 45 minutes in the heat to get to meet Elsa and Anna. (These are the stars of the *Frozen* movie franchise. You old people ask the grand kids about it.) She got to talk with the real

Elsa, her favorite, and have her picture taken with her. She hasn't stopped talking about that day these three years, and I hope she tells her grandkids about it one day.

We drove home leisurely, stopping at different campgrounds with pools. CC swam and told anyone who she came upon of the wonderful time she had in California. Disneyland and Uncle Rich's pool with the waterfall slide were her two favorite topics. I would build campfires and roast hot dogs and make smores. Guy would romp around the little dog parks and Grandma (the grandkids all call her Busha) would read a book enjoying her own solitude while we kids played. The only time I drove at night was the last day when Busha had enough of our sweet little rambunctious 6-year-old and asked me if I minded not stopping for the night and just getting home. I readily agreed and we got home around 10:00 p.m. Our West Coast trek was finished. We waited until the following day to unpack and clean out the RV, a nice hot long shower and our big soft bed awaited. AHHHH. Home at last.

Chapter Twenty: Workin' for the State

Summer and back on the job, I was given the task of operating the boom mower, and I loved it. I would spend the entire day cutting the high grass and weeds that the regular mowers couldn't reach. The best part was that I operated alone. I would download audiobooks to my phone and listen through headphones or earbuds all day while merrily chopping weeds and small bushes. (A far cry from the books on tape from back in the day.) I would even be farmed out to other yards to clean up their hard-to-reach weed patches. I would often have the chance for overtime at these other yards. This made for a nice summer. I didn't have to return to normal duty until it was time for fall inspection.

I now spent the months of September and October getting the yard's snow plows ready for inspection. I devised a method of dismantling the plows, welding any cracks that were found, repairing damaged parts, and re-assembling them with new bolts and springs. I even welded new lengths of chain that attached the plows to the lifting rams on the front of the trucks. How did I find myself doing the welding you ask? Well one weekend I asked the boss if I could use the truck bay to do a repair on my little trailer. He said, "Sure, as long as you clean up after yourself." On Saturday, I brought my trailer in and started work. I found a crack in my hitch assembly and prepared the metal for welding. As I was finishing my repair, the boss's voice startled me by saying, "You never told me you could weld." This was something I tried keeping to myself, but now it was common knowledge.

I was one of the old school welders who learned to weld with an arc welder and oxy acetylene back in high school. The state didn't issue MiG welders or plasma cutters to the yards. Every yard did have a stick welder and a set of tanks. I was drafted. Now every time something made of metal needed repair, I was summoned. I grew to like this new position. I would be left alone to work alone, as long as I got the job done. I found that if I was making sparks of any kind, people would keep their distance. I again donned my ear buds and made noise and sparks. I'd hammer pins and cut blocks. Most of the welding is taken up by preparing the metal. The welding part usually goes fast. Come on, who doesn't like playing with molten metal and getting paid for it?

The following snow and ice season found me volunteering for the night shift. The state decided that changing shifts back and forth throughout the winter was hard on people. Ya think??!! As soon as you would get used to nights, they would have you back on days. When that week was over, back to nights again. We didn't know if we were coming or going, to borrow a phrase. Night shift was great as far as I was concerned. Less traffic to deal with while plowing. More overtime too. Let me try to explain. If you get confused, it's okay, it took me about five years to sort of understand how the state works. (Nobody fully understands it.)

Here we go. During the snow and ice season, all highway maintainers will report for work at the normal 6:30 a.m. start time. They are to complete the tasks of the day. They will all be dismissed at 3:00 p.m., at which time the night shift will be on stand-by for possible callouts overnight. The first exception to this schedule is the *night patrol*. The night patrol consists of one driver and two trucks. (I know, it's starting to get confusing. How can one driver drive two trucks?) The primary truck was usually a small dump truck loaded with rock salt. You know, the stuff that melts ice and snow, while aiding in your car's depreciation value by rusting it away before your eyes. The driver patrols the entire team section, keeping his or her eyes peeled for road hazards, such as icy spots, non-functioning traffic lights, abandoned cars too close to the travel lanes, naked drunk people wandering around in the snow, and auto accidents. Each hour, a location and road conditions are relayed, via radio, to control up in Schaumburg. The secondary truck is also loaded with salt. This is a larger dump truck equipped with a plow designed to clear the roadways of accumulating snow that, if not removed promptly, will prove hazardous to the motoring public.

If the night patrol driver encounters the winter precipitation, this discovery is immediately reported to control. Radar is consulted, bosses are awakened, and after determining if this should be considered a real storm, or just a driver with dirty glasses and a wild imagination, the appropriate action is taken. This action ranges from calling out a few extra trucks and drivers supervised by a lead worker and a heavy equipment operator to load salt onto the trucks, to a full "All hands-on deck" call out of the entire night shift, who hopefully had a chance to rest up a bit after working till 3:00 p.m. that afternoon. Still puzzled on why there are two trucks assigned to night patrol? Me too.

The second exception to the 6:30 a.m. to 3:00 p.m. schedule comes at times when the powers that be up in Schaumburg listen to someone, besides the voices in their heads, and are apprised of an upcoming imminent threat of a snowstorm. At this time, some-one up there will issue orders for the night shift personnel to be sent home to rest at 10:30 a.m. and either await further orders or be given a time to report back to work. I like a good afternoon nap as much as the next man, but not after getting a full night's sleep, not even knowing whether I'll be called out at some unknown time. If I were to try to sleep all afternoon, sleep would elude me if not called in, making it difficult to function properly the next morning. If given specific orders to report at a fixed predetermined time however, I would close my room darkening curtains, lock the bedroom door, turn on the ceiling fan, insert earplugs, and crawl between the sheets. With my alarm set, and my phone on mute I would attempt slumber. I would arise and get dressed. I'd have dinner, fashioning a mid-shift meal of hot soup, a sandwich and some fruit. Coffee is of course essential. I was ready for a night of plowing, or salting, or sometimes driving around watching the sky waiting for the storm to start. It all paid the same.

Serving my time on night patrol was a joy for me. Patrol started at mid-night and lasted until 6:30 a.m. when the rest of the yard personnel showed up. Six-and-a-half hours of driving around, listening to a book, or the radio, all by myself. Here is another confusing area, to contemplate. Six-and-a-half hours worked, paid for a full 8-hour shift with one hour and 45 minutes which was called straight time overtime tossed in for good measure. I didn't want nor need to understand why, I just saw the extra overtime in my paycheck, and it was good. I also liked the only working six-and-a-half hours instead of the normal eight. Told you it was confusing.

Getting called out in the summertime for such hazards as rim busting potholes, trees down, or water on pavement complaints that are called in from time-to-time, usually takes around 30 minutes to an hour to complete. When called out, we would be required to get to the yard as fast as possible and get whatever equipment ready. When everyone who is called shows up, we head out to the complaint site. We quickly complete our nocturnal chore, returning to the yard with all haste. Signing out, we return home and try to get back to sleep, returning to work at 6:30 a.m. For these minor callouts, we receive three hours of overtime pay, even if the task only takes 30 minutes from getting up and dressed, to disrobing and crawling back into bed. Not a bad gig you say. I would agree most of the time. The times when we are called out at say 1:30 a.m., and end up working until 4:00 a.m., and are still required to be at work again at 6:30 a.m., would stretch one's ability to function properly. The older one gets the harder it is to work without sleep, (… at least that's what I've been told).

Things are calculated a little differently. Callouts still pay three hours, no matter how long a task may take. However, any task that occurs after midnight or starts before midnight and runs past midnight requires the person called out to remain on duty until 5:20 a.m. This person would then be off duty for the rest of the day, reporting at 6:30 a.m. the following day, unless there is a snowstorm or threat of a snowstorm. Then this individual would be required to report back to the yard as early as 4:00 p.m. and drive, salt, and plow for an overnight 12-and-a-half-hour shift. From 4:00 p.m. until midnight would be time-and-a-half overtime, midnight until 6:30 a.m. paid at the normal 8-hour shift rate with the one-and-three-quarter straight time over time. Are you still with me? If you were able to follow that, please explain it to me. My brain hurts when I try to calculate my hours. They could have been cheating me for years and I doubt if I could have caught such treachery.

Chapter Twenty-One: ...For Someone Your Age

I had my torn right shoulder rotator cuff, mentioned in the Hawaiian excursion, repaired before snow and ice season, the year I turned 59. I was told this was a significant tear that was most likely caused over time from the rigors of my prior work life. Driving big rigs, shifting gears, loading, and unloading freight and climbing around like a monkey hauling cars, could have had something to do with it. I was still in pretty good shape for my age. I worked at a physically demanding job (at times) and I worked out at the gym several days a week. I'd get through this with no worries. Shoulder surgery is no picnic. I was not prepared for this. Surgery isn't the problem, that's the doctor's problem. The recovery is what hits you like a baseball bat across the shins. The first part was the fact that the anesthesia deadened and debilitated the entire upper right-hand side of my body. Being immobilized is good for a shoulder that is being sliced, pinned, and stitched. Not so good for the muscles that operate the lung that lives on that side of one's chest cavity. This caused a bit of panic when I couldn't draw a deep breath. This passed just before the pain started and all thoughts of breathing flew out the window. I was also not ready for the pain. I thought I'd be a macho tough guy and resist taking the prescribed opiates. I found out that I am not that macho. After ingesting the proffered pills, I could feel the pain subside. I also became rather loopy which gave Nancy a well-deserved bit of amusement. While convalescing, I did have a tendency toward being whiny. Nancy never complained, at least not to my face.

Without the use of your right arm, simple tasks become extremely hard, if not impossible, (…unless of course you are left-handed). Dressing requires either assistance or being a contortionist. When you are used to eating right-handed, you occasionally miss the target, again becoming a source of entertainment for your spouse. Missing the target is also a concern with other aspects of life, such as the evacuation of one's bladder. You men out there try using the opposite hand than you are used to the next time the urge comes over you, have some paper towel and sanitary wipes handy. The other issue that we all handle in the bathroom is even more awkward and requires a great degree of concentration. I didn't even attempt shaving.

Physical therapy is a necessary evil. These therapists are all smiles and sweetness while they push and pull your healing stiff muscles. Smiling through gritted teeth, sweating, and trying not to let my pain show, I endured. Silently cursing and saying to myself, "Don't cry in front of the therapist, don't cry in front of the therapist." I endured this torture twice a week. I then rounded it out with my own therapy three more days a week, doing all the exercises taught to me by the sweet little sadist. I would follow the latter with a long soak in a jacuzzi at the gym. I weaned myself off the pain meds by this time. I worked very hard to get back to work before the snow started flying.

I finally convinced my doctor that I was fit to return to work. I had run out of sick days and vacation days, I even borrowed 10 sick days against next year. I needed to get back to work. On my return, I was awarded a lead worker position, temporary for the snow and ice season. This came with the use of a pickup truck, which allowed me to keep my BMW in the garage all winter. It also afforded me the opportunity to continue to recover and not do any physical labor until my strength returned. When I next visited my surgeon, he said he was impressed by my progress. Then added those hateful words, "For someone your age."

At this point I was 59. Okay, I couldn't run a marathon, but I could hold my own in most arenas. Maybe this was all in my mind, but I didn't think so. When the doctor told me I may never be 100%, I scoffed. I'm not going to settle for less. I'll see you in January and show you what I can do. I then asked him, "Doc, do you think I'll be able to play golf?" He replied, "Sure, you should have no problem with golf." At which time I hit him with the punchline, "That's great! I never could play golf before!" These surgeons have no sense of humor. I didn't even get a smirk.

On December 28th, I entered my gym, and signed up for my senior discount, this being my 60th birthday. I changed into my workout attire and hit the weight room. After warming up, I headed for the *big boy* weight bench. I asked for a spotter so as not to crush myself. I then proceeded to bench press 315 lbs.

Only twice, but I did it. This has no bearing on my story, I am just bragging.

The ears went first. Nancy noticed way before I was ready to admit that I may be a little hard of hearing. The TV was never loud enough, and most sentences had, 'What?' in them. I got Nancy a bedside clock that not only projected the time on the ceiling of our bedroom, but also produced the soothing sounds of a forest which is supposed to aid in slumber. This device also incorporated the chirping of cricket in the soothing forest sounds. One night while trying to nod off, I asked Nancy, "What happened to the crickets?" She answered, "The crickets are happily chirping their little heads off. Will you now have your ears checked?" I made an appointment with the VA and was examined by an audiologist. It was determined that along with significant hearing loss, mainly in the high range, I also was suffering from Tinnitus. This is the constant ringing in the ear that can drive one a little batty. I never knew what Tinnitus was, now I had it. There is nothing that can be done for Tinnitus that works, despite all the claims of the latest snake oil peddlers all over the Internet these days. So, I, along with millions of others suffer in, what we all wish was, silence.

I was issued a set of state-of-the-art, (I just love that phrase, especially when it is something I have.) of hearing aids. The batteries are recharged in a docking port on my nightstand. A necklace that accompanies this ensemble, pairs my hearing aids with my cell phone via Bluetooth wireless connection. This necklace can also be wirelessly paired to another device that hooks up with the TV. The necklace also controls the volume of my new hearing aids and has its own charging dock. Now I can listen to the TV without bothering Nancy or the neighbors down the block, with the excess volume of previous times. If Nancy goes to sleep first, I can turn the sound off on the TV and still enjoy whatever program I decide to fall asleep to. My audiobooks are also projected right into my head with these handy little devils. I do get some weird looks when I am talking on my phone with my necklace tucked in my shirt, with no visible device to be seen. "Mommy why is that man talking to himself?" Followed by, "It's not polite to point at crazy old men dear." I now say goodnight to the crickets when I place my hearing aid onto their charging ports.

My teeth have haunted me since my early years with the sadistic dentist who tried scaring children into brushing their teeth. Over the years, I had numerous cavities. I wore a retainer to help straighten the tusks that were my eye teeth. The removal of all four wisdom teeth, at the meaty hands of a particularly evil U.S. Navy dentist, was very painful as I recall. Excruciating also comes to mind. He did not prescribe the type of drugs that today's doctors pass out more liberally. Then there was the dental hack, who butchered a good portion of my lower teeth, installing crowns and caps, that cost the insurance company the price of sending his kids to Harvard. This was in California so, at least this guy used not only Novocain, but also twilight sleep and laughing gas. While under that happy trio, I would have agreed to let him play in my mouth to his heart's content. Just keep the drugs flowing Doc.

When I moved back to the Chicagoland area, I again found myself in need of dental assistance. My parents' dentist had retired and moved to Florida, living the high life on my parents' dime. I looked in the phone book and recognized a name from my earlier days at St. Francis of Rome. One of my former classmates was indeed a dentist. I made an appointment, and after combing my memory to see if there were any reasons for this kid to have a grudge to settle with me, I entered his office. We greeted each other as old friends and chatted a little about old classmates each of us kept in touch with over the years. This acted to both put my mind at ease about the whole possible vendetta thing and cemented a friendship. (He's still my dentist too.)

I have had the crowns, installed by the quack in California, fall out, get infected and then fall out, and start to hurt so bad that no amount of whiskey could numb the pain enough to allow sleep. Once, while driving through Ohio, one of these crowned teeth became abscessed. I was in pain, but I had to keep driving. Aspirin or aspirin powder was all I could take to try to relieve my agony. The crown now extricated itself from my abscessed tooth. After eating some soup for dinner, I was walking back to where the trucks were parked with another driver. I smelled something foul. I looked at my boots thinking that I stepped in something that dogs do outside. I didn't, neither did the other driver, who told me he didn't smell anything. This vial odor was emanating from my mouth, more accurately the festering tooth. I was one miserable truck driver, and I was still three states from home.

I delivered my load the next morning in Toledo. I called dispatch and through a clenched, now swollen jaw, shared the fact that I was driving home to get my tooth fixed or pulled. I didn't care if I was going to be fined. I didn't care if they wanted to cancel my lease. I was going home NOW. I didn't get fined, and my lease was still intact when I returned for duty. I was informed that my little tantrum was not uncommon at all. It was even considered as a request and not the threat I heard in my head. The pain was drowning out any sound that came out of my mouth. I immediately contacted my dental friend who immediately prescribed a strong antibiotic and a strong painkiller ready for me when I got home. The throbbing pain did not subside until that first blessed shot pierced my gums and the blinding agony lifted. The tooth could not be salvaged so I shrugged and let him yank it out; much less violently than the Naval sadist.

In subsequent years, I have had many root canals, a few new crowns, and two bridges installed. My top teeth, having suffered much the same trauma, were starting to deteriorate in much the same way that the bottom ones did. Instead of a bridge, which I was told would not work up there, I was fitted for a partial denture, consisting of the three teeth I was missing. This worked very well indeed, that is until two more of my upper crowns fell apart and couldn't be glued back into my head. I am now waiting for my mouth to heal after the offending teeth were extracted. I'll be heading back to have my friend take an impression of my remaining teeth and gums and have a new partial denture appliance made. I may be able to have a steak in a couple months. At least on my soft diet, I lost a few pounds.

The previous June, as I was working with a crew trenching next to the shipping canal, I lost my balance, and not wanting to fall into this less than pristine waterway, I grabbed the first handhold I could reach to try to stop my downward progress. I felt a twinge of agony tear into my left shoulder. I immediately knew what it was. I'm no doctor and I haven't played one for many years, but I knew the sensation radiating from my left shoulder. I had torn the other rotator cuff. Oh goody. I was taken to the local clinic where I filled out endless paperwork, was x-rayed, given orders to try to lift my arm, (which I failed to do for the nice doctor because it hurt) given a prescription, and an order to get an MRI. I was then sent back to work with further orders that would have me on light duty with no lifting or any other use of my left arm. I was ordered to wear a sling. The MRI showed that I did have a rotator cuff tear and, with the consensus of the doctor who repaired my right shoulder, that this shoulder also would require surgery. Okay, I knew what to expect this time so, let's get this thing scheduled so I can be ready for snow and ice season.

Murphy was back in the form of the insurance company in charge of Workers Compensation for the State of Illinois. After filling out reams of paperwork, and being poked and prodded by numerous other doctors, and being made to sit and do nothing, but still having to be at work every day, I finally secured an attorney. I wish I had thought about that sooner. He cut through red tape and went to bat for me. He had a date for surgery set for August. This was going to work. I should be recovered sufficiently to plow some snow and make some overtime this year. This sounds like a plan. Let's go.

This surgery was easier than the right side. At least that's what the doctor told me. I didn't know. I was asleep. Now I was home and didn't hesitate to take the prescribed goodies. I also didn't have to use any of my sick days or vacation days. I got hurt at work which was a two-edged sword as I would soon find out. I followed the doctor's orders and got as much exercise as I could manage. I walked to and from my physical therapy sessions, avoiding the donut shop both ways. I worked almost as hard as I did the first go around. I figured I'd be back to work in November, I figured wrong. Due to this being a Workers Comp case, I would not be released for my return to work, until the full healing process completed. Okay, I can deal with this if the checks keep coming. December rolled around and I was still not allowed to return to work. January turned into February and finally my surgeon released me for full duty. I was ready to get back to work. Hold your horses, now you must be evaluated by our independent doctor who will make the final decision. Another three weeks and I got to visit this esteemed physician. I passed his exam and was finally certified ready to go back to full duty. A full 10 months after my injury. The checks did keep coming so I guess I shouldn't complain. There wasn't much of a winter so there were not a lot of overtime hours to be had.

I reported back for full duty March 10th. I was assigned to a litter picking crew. It was March and it was cold. I'm now thinking, maybe I should have faked my range of motion in that last test and waited for warmer weather. I kept bundled up, listened to a book, and picked up the discarded refuse tossed out of car windows by lazy people who pay us to pick up after them. After two weeks of this fun, it was my turn for night patrol. Since I hadn't had the chance to be on night patrol all winter and there were only two weeks left in the season, I would get the last two weeks. Also, these were the early days of the Coronavirus pandemic of 2020.

So, isolating the *at-risk* had just started. I, being a senior citizen, needed to be isolated from the rest of the crew. (I honestly believe Nancy and I had this potentially deadly virus back in February. Both of us had all the symptoms of the pandemic virus. Neither of us remembers being that sick for that long since childhood.) I accepted this plum and spent the next two weeks sleeping days and driving nights and thinking over my options. There was a brief late season snowstorm that blew in over the Sunday that would start my last night patrol week. I got the call to report at 3:00 p.m. Sunday afternoon. The storm was cancelled at 10:30 p.m. Everyone went home. Everyone, except me. I had to stay and perform my night patrol duty until 6:30 a.m. Monday morning.

Chapter Twenty-Two: Retire, Remodel, Regroup

Somewhere around 4:00 a.m. on Monday March 24th, a flicker of an idea formed in my sleep deprived brain. Over the next few nights, I developed this flicker into a full-fledged plan, and on Friday morning, the last day of night patrol, I informed the boss that I would be taking the following Monday off as a personal day.

I then called and made an appointment with the payroll lady, who helped me with my transfer 9-and-a-half years earlier. I drove up to Schaumburg, and sat myself down and asked my question, "What would it take for me to retire?" There, I said it out loud. I had, of course, discussed it with Nancy, who was supportive asking only if we could afford it. She then reminded me that grandkids would be under foot a lot, (Busha is the designated grandbaby watcher when mom and dad must work.) and I should enter that into my equation before making a final decision.

After consulting her computer and retrieving a file from across the office, she said to me, "You have the time, and you are certainly old enough. I can fill out the paperwork right now and you can be retired on Wednesday, April 1st." Wow! I was really going to do it. I had practiced retirement from August 'til now, but now it was going to be official. I was happy and scared to death at the same time, kind of like when your kids are born.

I built my basement shower room, known by all as the men's room. (The third and fourth grade granddaughters call it the boy's room, and when any of them need to use it, giggle profusely.) I had constructed the walls and ceiling several years before. I plumbed it for a shower, sink, and toilet so that part was already in place. The shower stall was a cheap plastic affair that was less efficient than advertised. I did not like it, but I figured I could hold off on remodeling for a little while. Murphy accelerated my timeline.

Nancy went into the basement bathroom, probably to pilfer some of my hidden stash of toilet paper. She noticed there was water in the floor that was dripping from the soaked drywall of the ceiling. Oh goody. I tore down the sodden drywall and found my leak. A length of copper pipe had, out of the blue, developed a pin hole. This was not at a soldered joint; this was not where a nail or screw could have accidentally pierced it during my earlier construction. This was in the middle of a five-foot length of copper pipe. I think one of Murphy's minions was playing with an ice pick. New copper pipe was purchased, along with the proper connectors and hangers. This was completed quickly, because the water in the entire house had to be turned off while I repaired the leak. No water, no toilets. Lots of crossed legs and fidgeting, and the cry of, "Are you almost done yet?" Several trips to the local hardware store were involved and I decided to install an extra water shut off that would just shut off in the basement bathroom. (Don't tell anybody, but I used the restroom at the hardware store. How do you spell relief?)

Catastrophe diverted, I set about the task of remodeling the downstairs bathroom. I drew a blank. Nancy and I roamed the isles of our local big box hardware do-it-yourself store, and I was suffering from bathroom overload. I decided I should take care of the demolition of the damaged ceiling and one of the walls. I tore out the cheap shower stall. I ripped out the tile, removed the sink/ vanity, and toilet. I had a blank slate to work with, but what did I want to build? It came to me all at once. I would build a rustic, man cave, a fortress of solitude where I could hide away, if only briefly, from the estrogen laden rooms in the rest of the house. The toilet and sink/vanity would be fine, along with the mirror/medicine cabinet. The rest of the design had to come from me. I purchased bricks and mortar and outlined where the shower would be. I never did any brick work, so I was pleasantly surprised at how well this turned out. I then built a half wall out of 2x4s.

Now for the fun part. I bought 1x6 and 1x4 planks, just plain construction grade wood made of pine. I picked out the least attractive wood that I could find. (If this was a do-it-yourself reality show, I would have searched for an old farmer who was selling old barn planks to be repurposed, but this is real and not reality TV.) After coating these with a good marine varnish, I cut them to length. These planks were now secured to the ceiling, the wall where the sink/vanity, and my half wall, with screws made for outdoor decks. Next came my pride and joy. I ordered sheets of corrugated galvanized steel. The wall that the toilet was in front of, and the entire shower enclosure was clad in this steel. This was going to be cool.

Nancy came down as I was fastening the ceiling planks and asked me why I was using wood instead of drywall. I told her it was because if I needed to get to another plumbing disaster, I could unscrew the planks and access the pipes and not have to patch drywall. At his point, she pointed at the ceiling and said, "You mean like that leak right there?" I looked up and, sure enough, I had pierced the same copper pipe that started this whole mess with a screw. When I removed the offending screw, water came gushing out between the planks, giving me my first shower in my new man cave. With my new valve, at least I didn't have to shut off the water in the entire house and could work on this repair at my leisure. If I could have calculated and measured where this pipe was, I don't think I could have stabbed it with any more accuracy. I hit it dead on. A few more trips to the hardware store and, once again, had functioning plumbing. I now designed my shower itself. I decided on bare galvanized pipe, and plain faucet handles and a plain, but serviceable shower head. I further built the shower curtain and even the toilet paper holder out of this same pipe. I hung hooks for my hair and beard dryers, installed a shelving unit over my toilet, and hung a metal Harley sign. (This is where Santa fixes his beard. You gotta keep reading for the explanation.) My man cave shower came out great if I do say so myself. Nancy was also impressed with my ingenuity. I've come a long way from the days of Grandpa standing naked in the basement under a makeshift shower. I'm sure he's looking down at my mancave and saying, "Ima wisha I hada one of those."

The VA scheduled a sleep study for me back in February. I spent the night at Hines Veterans Hospital where I was hooked up to machines via wires taped and glued to various places on my body. I had a contraption strapped to my chest and oxygen tubes taped to my face with two tubes shoved up my nose. Now I was supposed to sleep in an unfamiliar room in a bed that wasn't mine, without Nancy next to me? Not an easy task to accomplish. I had been having trouble sleeping for some time now and this exam was supposed to shed light on this problem. I was allowed to take my sleep medication prescribed by my psychiatrist and the room was equipped with a TV, so I settled in and watched the local news. I eventually nodded off because the next thing I knew, the nurse was in the room checking a monitor and adjusting one of my wires. She said to me, "I'm not sure who snores louder, you or the gentleman in the next room." I could hear him sawing logs through the wall behind my head. I smiled through my medicated haze and dropped back off to sleep. In the morning I was able to wash most of the goo from my face, (not an easy task with my full beard) got dressed and exited the hospital in search of coffee and breakfast. The results of my test wouldn't be ready for a week or so. I would wait patiently for the results. This came a few weeks later, with a phone call advising me that I was to report back to Hines where a doctor would make a further evaluation of my condition. An appointment was made, and I again ventured over to Hines. I was still off work convalescing, so no problem.

Upon arrival, I was ushered into a conference room already occupied with other vets who had also been subject to the same sleep study that I endured. The doctor came in and informed us that we all had sleep apnea and would be now issued machines to fix this sleep disorder. Okay, I'll give this a try, what can it hurt? We were then talked through what sleep apnea was and how it affected our health. This was some scary stuff. The number of times we had stopped breathing, as shown on the numerous monitors we had been hooked up to while sleeping, was shocking. Then it was explained that the lack of oxygen to our bodies was hurting our hearts and other organs. We were not getting a refreshing, revitalizing, restful sleep we needed to function properly during the day. This also explains why I would be drowsy and nod off so often during the day.

Okay, I get it, oxygen good, not breathing bad. We were trained in the proper use of our CPAP apparatuses. I, thank God, didn't have to wear the full-face mask, due to my beard which didn't allow for a tight seal. Instead, I was fitted with a smaller soft rubber tubular device that was surprisingly comfortable. This tube thing fits over my head, under my nose, and is held in place with a soft elastic band that goes around the back of my head. At the very top, there is another long flexible tube attached to both my head tube and the machine on my nightstand. This took a lot of getting used to. Being conscious of my breathing made it difficult to fall asleep. I found that I would remove the apparatus from my head in the middle of the night without remembering a thing. This may be due to my *night, night* drugs. I eventually got used to this new nightly ritual and started to sleep better than I had in years. (Decades probably, but who's counting.) The first thing I noticed was that my ribs stopped hurting. This was because I wasn't getting poked and told to roll over by my loving spouse. Did I mention I used to snore? The second thing I noticed was that I wasn't sleepy during the day! I wouldn't nod off in the afternoon. Now that I'm retired and free to take afternoon naps, I don't have the need for one. I'm not sure if that's good or bad.

Chapter Ummm: I Don't Remember, I'm Getting Older

I am now Santa Claus. (Okay, not the real Santa, I'm one of his trusted helpers.) I knew this full white beard would come in handy for something. I am pretty good at being Santa. I bought a very plush, and expensive Santa suit. My motorcycle boots equipped with white fur on the top adds to the realism. I even bought round Santa glasses. Nancy made me a plush Santa bag. That is where she draws the line. She refuses to dress up as Mrs. Claus. I am destined to be a solo act. After surfing the web, I purchased a fake Santa tummy. I'm not thin, but I needed help filling out the suit. Karen came to my aid by designing business cards for me that show my big Santa smile and boasts of my real beard. (I've only had a couple little darlings test the realness of my facial hair.) I have no plans to be a mall Santa, I instead do private events and parties. There are a couple of websites I use to book Santa gigs, and I have a ball being the jolly old elf. I am enrolled in Santa College in the fall. I hope to learn more about entertaining as the big guy. I'll be able to get tips on my HO HO HOing, and how to whiten the parts of my beard that persist in staying darker gray.

I thought I was a star visiting my old high school, but this was a special kind of stardom that shows on the face of children. I know and cherish the true meaning of Christmas. I know Santa is or at least should be, a second thought. If bringing joy into the lives of small children isn't what Jesus would do, I'll turn in my jingle bells and shave my face. I am hired for in-home family parties, and school events. I entertain at adult parties too, where I pass out gag gifts and sing carols with the revelers. When I'm asked, I visit sick children in hospitals. I don't charge for these visits, the brightness and hope coming from the faces of children and adults is more than enough pay for this Santa.

The most heart-breaking event I was asked to do as Santa was for a request from The *Make-A-Wish Foundation*. I was to show up at a grade school assembly to make a presentation to an 8-year-old girl with cancer. She and her family were being awarded a trip for four to Disney World, all expenses paid. When I entered, the children were already singing *Here Comes Santa Claus*, and the squeals reached a decibel level to rival any heavy metal concert. The little girl had no idea what was going to happen. She was just enjoying the singing and Santa's entrance. I spoke a few words and let out a few hearty Ho Ho Hos and motioned for quiet. Children always obey when Santa speaks. I called the name of the girl, who was clearly surprised, and invited her to join me at the center of the gym floor. Now from the other side of the room, her parents and older brother came in. The *Make-A-Wish* spokesperson slipped in while the little family did some hugging. When the spokesperson made the announcement of the award, the noise level erupted to an even louder level than before. Tears were everywhere. I think even old St. Nick had a few on his rosy, red cheeks too.

Nancy took a picture of me while on a Santa break last year. I had removed my coat and hat. I was reclining on our sofa. I was clad in my red pants, fur accented boots, a large white long-sleeved tee shirt, red suspenders, and my Santa tummy (under the T-shirt.) The caption could have read, "The day after Christmas." Nancy sent the picture to Karen, who cleaned it up, and added some extra decorations. Karen then had this masterpiece framed and sent it to me as a birthday present. I was touched. Looking at it now, I kick myself for not including a bottle of Coke in my hand. (A bottle of Bud Light might have worked too.) Could have made for a nice schmaltzy Holiday ad. *Yo Coke people, have your people call my people and we'll do lunch.*

I am in a band again. Fun stuff. Gives me more to do. A while back, the trombone player from my old swing band called me. We chatted a bit and reminisced about the old days. Then he asked me if I would be interested in helping some friends of his struggling with the management of their band. I listened as he explained their problems and lack of leadership. When he told me they would be open to including a sax player/singer to the band, he had me hooked. He gave my information and I copied down the current head man of this band. I dusted off my horns and started the process of getting my chops back. (This, for all you non-musicians out there, means practice.)

I found a new friend in YouTube. I could pull up a variety of music and play along. In earlier days, a band would make up cassette tapes for the musicians to practice with. (Yes, this was the stone age before CDs and MP3s and other newfangled ways of recording music. Okay, you snickering young folks, OFF THE LAWN!) The only problem with these was the fact that not all cassette players were the same. If the recording was made on a recorder that had, say weak batteries and the one the tape was played back on had a fresh set of batteries, the key would not be the same. Musicians like myself who play mostly by ear would practice the key they heard and not the key the band was playing in. You can see how this could be difficult and frankly, very frustrating.

I found and printed out lyrics that I would need to sing. I never had to memorize lyrics because, first, I sang at church and always had a song book or sheet music to follow. Second, I played a wind instrument, and try as I might, I never could figure out how to do both at the same time. I never even learned the words to my high school fight song; I was too busy trying to play the right notes on my clarinet, well, that and checking out the cheerleader types frolicking and bouncing all over the place. Don't judge me, you were in high school once.

I was ready to meet the guys. I drove out to Flossmoor, Illinois. Nice neighborhood. The band was set up in the basement. I met the Bass player *Red;* drummer *Tweet;* lead guitar *Fingers;* and second guitar *Rick.* We haven't come up with a nickname for him yet. All very good musicians. I wasn't sure I was good enough to play with these guys. (I never think I'm a good enough musician. Who does?) We jammed for a while, and right away I found the problem. Nobody was in charge. It took several minutes just to settle on one song to play. Everyone had his own ideas on what key to play in. I was silent at this point; I just met these guys. When asked what I thought, I took a deep breath and said, "Well you guys sound good and you really know how to play. If you want to sound great and want me to join, we have to start playing together as a unit." The guys agreed. I went further saying, "We need to practice at home on our own, and when we come together, we are here to rehearse." I had their attention; they now saw me as a leader. We needed a solid four-set list that we would polish until we could play without a hitch. We needed to name this band. We needed to present a professional brand if we wanted to play in public. We jammed a bit more and the night ended with enthusiastic hopes for the next rehearsal. I wasn't sure if I was accepted or merely tolerated. I drove home not having a clue if I would see those guys ever again.

I received three calls the very next day. The first was from Rick, who asked if I was interested in being in the band. I said, "Yes, I would love to," and we made plans for our next rehearsal. My apprehension started fading. Second call was from Tweet, who also extended an invitation to work on this project together. He was doing most of the singing at this point and knows a lot more about the technical side of music. (Strange for a drummer. Just kidding, lots of musically inclined drummers out there.) The third call came from my old trombone friend. He told me that the guys were very impressed with my ideas and were also extremely impressed with my musical talent. Wow! To be hailed like this was a major boost to my ego.

I started working *full steam ahead* on as many aspects of band forming as I could think of. By the next rehearsal, I was ready to go. I lugged what I call my heavy metal over to Rick's basement. This was comprised of four saxophones (Soprano, Alto, Tenor, and Baritone), music stand, stands for all four horns, microphone stand, my amp, my six-pack of harmonicas, my cordless mic setup for the horns, a gig bag with notebooks and binders full of song lyrics, vocal mics, a variety of cords and, my musical offerings. I couldn't load it all in my car, so I hooked up my motorcycle/utility trailer up to the Jeep and drove the 30 miles to Rick's house. Unloading and navigating the narrow staircase leading to the basement was a chore. Good thing I had some help. Making several trips with all that heavy stuff would have left me without much breath left to blow my horns. Setting up my equipment took some time, and I got to know the guys as I worked. We agreed on rehearsing several songs that the guys knew. I then asked each of them to think up a band name so we could talk about it after rehearsal. After much debate, which lasted over an hour, we decided on several options. It was further decided that we take the week and mull over these names. I did Google searches and whittled the list down to three. With a vote the following Friday night and landed on *Southside Soul Kings*. We were headed forward in first gear, slowly.

I then reached out to my talented sister Karen, (Okay Gina and Ann, you are also talented.) to help with a logo for the band. After several attempts, we came up with a very professional logo. Southside Soul Kings took another step forward. I had a banner and a bass drum sign made. It looks fabulous, baby. Next, I hired a photographer and had band pictures taken. We all wore black suits and red shirts. We were stylin'. Now it was time to look for gigs to book. With my previous experience in booking the swing band, I felt confident that I could get this new venture off the ground. I booked a few gigs at my local American Legion, and we had our first paying job. We were not polished, but the crowd had a good time. Yes, alcohol was involved, but that makes us sound better. We were asked to return for the Memorial Day picnic. This was great! I invited friends and family.

Karen and Rich were in town visiting friends and family, so they were able to attend. We were having a blast going through our set list and getting the patrons dancing and singing along. Halfway through our second set, the sky opened, the rain poured, and the wind blew in with a vengeance. We were inside the pavilion so, with the doors closed we kept playing. All at once everyone's cell phones started a wailing alarm that pierced right through our music. The announcement stopped the show. A tornado warning was in place for the very spot we were in. Everyone was instructed to move inside the main building where there was better shelter. We mingled with our fans and heard nothing but praise. Our egos got a nice shot in the arm. There was even a video posted on Facebook showing off our talent. It was an iPhone recording, but the sound came through just fine. I was ready to start looking for other bookings. We were not looking to get rich or make a gold record deal, we just wanted to entertain audiences, and have fun doing it.

Murphy likes messing with musicians too. In early June, I had my mishap at work that eventually led to my shoulder surgery. Fingers injured his leg, leading to his own hospitalization. Tweet had another malady that kept him from the drum set all summer. We were determined to carry on with our project. This would be a temporary setback; we would weather the storm. We weren't in a hurry. Summer gigs were out of the question, so we set our sights on fall and winter. Well spring (yes, spring) came around and we were all healthy. I had applied for several spring and summer events and festivals. We were ready at last to entertain the population.

Murphy again enters the picture. This time on a global scale. Whether you call it the pandemic virus, or the China bug, it stopped the world cold. The global pandemic snuck up and bit us in the hind end. We were told to shelter in place. Don't go outdoors unless absolutely necessary. Wear a mask in public. Businesses were shut down. Schools were closed. Bars and restaurants were boarded up. March turned into April, with predictions of even longer self-quarantine. Slogans of "Stay home. Stay safe." were plastered all over. The media fed this worldwide fear of germs. The craziest thing, to me at least, was the hoarding of toilet paper. Stocking up on food and sanitizing cleaners I could understand. Toilet paper? The stores ran out of the very useful paper products virtually overnight. People were buying several cases at once and going back for more. This caused store owners to start rationing. "I may not have food, but I sure can poop a lot." Essential workers such as truck drivers and factories that made paper products were exempt from the stay-at-home edict. They were making and transporting toilet paper to people. Okay I'll get down from my soapbox.

All the gigs I had scheduled for the spring were cancelled. We were looking towards the summer. We would be playing again in June, we thought. Wrong again. The stay-at-home order was extended. Now our state's governor aligned with the Mayor of Chicago, decided to cancel all the fairs, festivals, and virtually any other fun gathering of people that would have afforded the masses to enjoy our music, for the rest of the summer and possibly until the end of the year. I keep plugging away, sending out email after email to prospective venues. I have learned a lot since my earlier Swing Club Internet fiasco. We have a few band gigs in the near future to look forward to. We aren't letting a little global pandemic get us down. Southside Soul Kings will keep on makin' music.

Last Chapter for Now: I Ain't Dead Yet

Retired and managing my honey-do list a little at a time, there are a few hobby type projects that I'm working on. Refurbishing garden benches is one. I completed the bench we had in the backyard that was rotting and rusted. I shaped and sanded new slats, and wire brushed the rust off the metal parts, then stained the wood parts and painted the metal parts a nice Cubby Blue. (Sorry Bill and John and the rest of the Sox fans out there.) The bench came out so nice that I'll be branching out, refurbishing for friends. I even bought a dilapidated bench online to fix up and sell. I made a wind chime for Nancy out of an old fire extinguisher. I have an old high-pressure tank that is not certifiable any longer. As soon as I can figure out how to hang it, Nancy will have wind chimes that go bong, instead of tinkle, tinkle.

Riding motorcycles with the Legion Riders; playing in the band; being Santa; singing at church on Sundays; trying to get away with Nancy in our motorhome; writing this book; what else can I do to keep busy? I stopped playing golf when Dad died; I was always a triple-digit golfer and it's very expensive these days. (I only played to have the chance to spend more time with him.) I'm terrible at fishing. Maybe bowling? (If they ever open the bowling alleys after the pandemic virus runs its course.) Certainly, no sport that requires running. I don't run anymore. I don't see the need. I'm not in a hurry to get anywhere. When asked, "What if someone is chasing you?" I reply, "If someone is chasing me, it is certain they will catch me. By then I would be out of breath and too tired to fight back. Besides, if they are armed, I can't outrun a bullet anyway." Maybe politics? (Nancy is trying to steer me away from that crazy arena.) I am 66 years young. I have lots-o-time and there are lots of things I could do. There are places I haven't been to, and places I'd like to visit again. Tearing Nancy away from grandkids is one of my biggest challenges. (I don't think I'll ever be able to convince her to move a little south and a little east, where land is cheaper, and taxes are less.) There are more songs to learn and more people to entertain. There are more smiles to put on more children's faces, and more joy to bring to all at Christmas.

Where do I go from here? Well, I know where my keys are, most of the time. I'm sleeping better than I have since I was a kid. I can still lift heavy stuff. I need to keep being Bapa, and fixing things for the grandkids. There will be a need in the future for me to dance at weddings. There will be graduations to help celebrate, joyful times to be shared with friends and family. Unfortunately, there will be times to mourn the passing of old friends not as fortunate as I am in the health department. There will be lives to celebrate and accomplishments to share. There will be more Marvel movies that Nancy and I can enjoy together. (My Nancy sure likes Thor.) There will be more sunsets to become enthralled with. There is an aurora borealis to witness, gape jawed and awestruck. We hope there will be new grandbabies to welcome into the world. (Paul, this is aimed at you. Time's-a-wastin.' You ain't getting any younger.) There are fish boils in Door County, Wisconsin to share. Nancy wants to visit Hershey, Pennsylvania for the chocolate, and Vermont to visit and sample as much Ben and Jerry's as possible. We must see how the progress on the Crazy Horse monument is coming along. We have friends and family all over the country to drop in on. Baseball spring training is on next year's agenda, after experiencing Mardi Gras. We will marvel at the hot air balloon launch over Albuquerque, New Mexico one of these Octobers. I love telling my grandkids stories from my past, as well as stories I have read about from the past. I love telling old jokes to young people who weren't around the first time I told them. I also dutifully laugh at old jokes told by the young ones who heard them for the first time somewhere else.

I keep on trying to learn new things all the time. Albert Einstein once said, "When we stop learning, we start dying." His words keep me striving for knowledge. History is more fascinating the closer I am to being a part of it. There is a lot of living to do, and with the grace of God, I will have the chance to keep exploring.

Not The End!